The Plimoth Plantation
NEW ENGLAND COOKERY BOOK

W9-AWI-009

The Plimoth Plantation

THE HARVARD COMMON PRESS
HARVARD AND BOSTON
MASSACHUSETTS

NEW ENGLAND COOKERY BOOK

Malabar Hornblower
with the staff of Plimoth Plantation

The Harvard Common Press
535 Albany Street
Boston, Massachusetts 02118

Copyright © Plimoth Plantation Inc.

All rights reserved. No part of this publication may be reproduced or transmitted in any form or by any means, electronic or mechanical, including photocopy, recording, or any information storage or retrieval system, without permission in writing from the publisher.

Printed in the United States of America

Library of Congress Cataloging-in-Publication Data

Hornblower, Malabar.
   The Plimoth Plantation New England Cookery Book / Malabar Hornblower with the staff of Plimoth Plantation.
       p.   cm.
   Includes bibliographical references (p.   ) and index
   ISBN 1-55832-028-8: $19.95.—ISBN 1-55832-027-X: $9.95
   I. Cookery, American—New England style.   I. Plimoth Plantation, Inc.   II. Title.   III. Title: New England cookery book.
TX715.2.N48H67   1990
641.5974—dc20   90-5269
                                                          CIP

Cover photo by Glenn Kramer
Food styling for cover photo by John Carafoli
Cover design by Joyce Weston
Text design by Linda Ziedrich

10   9   8   7   6   5   4   3   2   1

This book is dedicated
in loving memory
to
Henry Hornblower II
(1917–1985)
founder
of
Plimoth Plantation

Contents

Acknowledgments

Although it may sometimes be true that too many cooks spoil the broth, this certainly isn't so in the case of *The Plimoth Plantation New England Cookery Book*. It has been a communal effort and a veritable labor of love on the part of many.

I cannot individually thank all the friends and members of Plimoth Plantation who gave me suggestions, lent me old, thumb-worn family cookbooks and parted with cherished recipes; the list would be too long. I am indebted to the men and women on the Plantation's staff—especially Troy Creane and Carolyn Freeman Travers—who worked long hours "translating," testing and retesting Native American and seventeenth-century recipes, making them viable for twentieth-century tastes and cooks while remaining true to their original concepts. Jim Baker, director of museum operations, was invaluable, not only for his articulate and scholarly chapters on Native American and seventeenth-century food styles, but for his overall knowledge of things historical and culinary. Finally, a heartfelt thanks to Diane Nottle, a longtime associate, who helped me test many of the "modern" recipes and organize the contents of the book.

M. H.

I
Introduction

Like any other cuisine, be it national or regional, New England's is the product of its land, its people and its history.

Although New England is comprised of six states, in essence it is one. Villages in Connecticut, with their white church steeples, look much the same as ones in Maine. The topography may differ slightly. Massachusetts's rolling, rock-encrusted fields contrast vividly with the timber-rich, eroded mountains of Vermont and New Hampshire, but wherever one can find a fertile pocket of land, much the same produce grows. In the south and east, New England is bordered by the sea—some of it, like Long Island Sound, Nantucket Sound and Cape Cod Bay, are large tracts of generally tranquil water, lapping at sandy shores. On the north, however, the ocean, whipped by winds, throws itself against the rocky promontories of Cape Ann and Maine. To the west, the Green Mountains of Vermont, the Berkshire Hills of Massachusetts and the Litchfield Hills of Connecticut, and beyond them the wide and mighty Hudson River, all act as a natural barrier against the rest of the United States. New England stands removed and isolated.

Climate is another unifying factor. It is not kind. Springs are usually nonexistent, summers are short—most New England gardeners consider themselves fortunate if their tomatoes ripen by mid-August—and winters harsh. Only the fall, extending well into November, is generous, with repeated intervals of sunny days whose warmth is visually enhanced by the glorious, justifiably famous coloring of the autumn leaves. While the summer brings us all the familiar crops—the tender peas of late June, to start, the green and yellow beans, globular purple beets, shiny eggplant, squash, zucchini, carrots, red and yellow tomatoes and ears of sweet young corn, to say nothing of wild and cultivated berries—it is in the fall, actually, that New England's produce comes into its own. After the first mild frost, the roadside stands peak with brilliant displays. Mounds of vivid pumpkins compete for attention with tan, orange and dark green winter squash, variegated gourds, squat turnips, elongated parsnips and barrels of ruby red apples—with their companion jugs of freshly squeezed cider. Fall in New England is harvesttime, but, more important, a time of stockpiling for the cruel months ahead.

New England's soil may be poor—most of the fertile top soil was scraped away by the advance and retreat of four successive glaciers—but its surrounding seas compensate the land with a plethora of riches. From the very beginning, the early explorers, who had, almost literally, bumped into America, returned to Europe with reports of a vast sea "covered with fish"—fish so plentiful they could be caught simply by lowering a basket into the water. English navigator Bartholomew Gosnold, nosing around New England in 1602 looking for sassafras (which he found in quantity, as, 20 years later, the Pilgrims did), chanced on a great hook of land that he named Cape Cod after all the cod he found swimming in the waters. Nor were cod and haddock, striped bass and bluefish, flounder and eels the only yield in the sea. There were shellfish in profusion. And, although no longer so plentiful, they are still there, and New Englanders feast on them.

It was the fruit of the sea, and the local Indians, that enabled the Pilgrims, the first permanent white settlers of the New England coast, to survive their first, nearly disastrous, winter of 1620–21. The land must have looked pretty bleak when they arrived at Plymouth harbor in late December on the 106$\frac{1}{2}$-foot Mayflower after a four months' voyage. Their supplies were low, and that first winter took a heavy toll: Half of the settlers died. But the sea nourished them as best it could, as did the wild game, and a friendly Indian named Squanto taught them the ways of the land.

"[He] was a speciall instrument sent of God for ther good beyond their expectation," wrote William Bradford in his chronicle, *Of Plimoth Plantation*. "He directed them how to set their corne, where to take fish, and to procure other comodities, and was also their chief pilott to bring them to unknowne places for their profitt, and never left them till he dyed."

The Pilgrims survived, the first of a hardy lot of tenacious souls who came and tilled the soil, cut the lumber, sailed the seas and worshiped God in their own way. As historian James Truslow Adams wrote, "The gristle of conscience, work, thrift, shrewdness, duty, became bone."

Plimoth Plantation, the living history museum of seventeenth-century Plymouth, is dedicated to telling the Pilgrims' story. It is a recreation of the Pilgrim village as it might have been seen in 1627, when the first hard years had been endured and the little colony was struggling to its feet. It is staffed by modern men and women who assume specific roles of seventeenth-century residents of Plimoth Colony. As visitors to the Plantation watch and, almost unconsciously, become a part of that former world, the "interpreters" pursue the daily, ofttimes ordinary, tasks of colonial life, all the while speaking in dialects of seventeenth-century English. Fields are planted, roofs are thatched, trees are felled, animals are tended, fires are watched—and food is prepared, seventeenth-century food cooked with the produce and materials of the past, in the manner of the past, with the tools of the past.

That same basic English cookery is the core, the foundation, of traditional New England food as it is known today. But it is a cuisine that has changed and evolved with the times. New England never remained indifferent to the waves of immigrants that swept through its ports, bringing their own foods and culinary styles. It happily assimilated them. New England's food, like the rest of the country's, is the sum of its multifaceted parts.

To rejoice in that mixed heritage, and to celebrate Plimoth Plantation's nearly half-century as one of the leading outdoor museums in the country, the Plantation decided to publish this book.

The Plimoth Plantation New England Cookery Book is not the first New England cookbook, nor, undoubtedly, will it be the last. But we have attempted to make it the best. We have taken New England's classic English dishes—never forgetting the Italian, Irish and Portuguese influences—and updated them to appeal to current tastes. To illustrate how remarkably good seventeenth-century English and Native American fare were, we are including two chapters devoted exclusively to recipes of the period. The rest of the book is strictly twentieth-century. We have been true to the essence, the flavor, of the original, but we bow to the public's current desire for lighter fare and ease of preparation. We have made every attempt to provide the best recipes we can research and devise, and, since many of today's cooks are concerned with time, we have noted at the beginning of each recipe how long it will take to prepare. Obviously the times given are rough estimates (leaning towards the high side), for some cooks are more adept at certain chores than others.

Recipes and tastes change over the years, and *The Plimoth Plantation New England Cookery Book* reflects the current mode. Squash soup is a good example. It was a big favorite in the seventeenth century, but through the years it was gradually eclipsed by more conventional soups and broths. Now, thanks perhaps to a more health-conscious, vegetable-oriented society, squash and pumpkin soups are back in favor.

In some ways, we've come full circle.

II

English Yeoman Foodways at Plimoth Plantation

BY JAMES W. BAKER
Director of Museum Operations at Plimoth Plantation

The popular image of colonial foodways is one of pioneer self-reliance reveling in no-nonsense, simple and wholesome recipes that used only the ingredients of a bountiful New World. The early settlers, for all their problems, did send back stories of seas, forests and fields full of the wild bounty of an unspoiled Eden, augmented by gardens brimming with vegetables. It became a truism among historians that arrival in this gastronomic paradise immediately released dormant instincts among the early colonists to joyously embrace a simple, natural diet. But it is a serious misreading of culture to think that the tastes of the period could change overnight. By the 1800s, it appears, a change in fashion had brought about a popularity for plain fare, but this was not true in the early 1600s. There was then no urge to move to simplicity, which is a value that conforms more to our ideals than to theirs.

This chapter is adapted from lectures given by James W. Baker at the Dublin Seminar for New England Folklife and at Radcliffe College's 1985 Conference on Current Research in Culinary History.

The community that Plimoth Plantation represents is a small English agricultural settlement set on the edge of the New World. Its crucial task is survival. The visitor witnesses mainly the performance of daily household tasks, in which, as was the case in 1627, foodways—the whole cycle of acquiring, processing and consuming food—play the central role.

The twentieth-century visitor enters a village that appears to be functioning for its own benefit, its own survival in the year 1627, rather than for the benefit of the visiting public. There are no tasks repeated as demonstrations of "how they would have done it," but rather as chores and work that must be done in any farming community if it is to prosper. What the visitor sees depends on the season, the time of day and the actual needs of the villagers.

At the Plantation, every house manned on a particular day has its cooking fire and evidence of some meal being, or having been, prepared and eaten. These are not treated as demonstrations to be interpreted or repeated, but as actual meals. Whenever possible, the materials are gathered in the village's own pens, gardens and fields, and prepared on site. Thus time is actually seen to pass; the villagers do not demonstrate regardless of the time of day or season.

The Mayflower carried about one hundred passengers, of whom half died within the first five months. Presumably the ship's stores lasted the 1621 season, but for fresh food it was necessary to forage for groundnuts, jerusalem artichokes and other wild plants; catch fish; gather shellfish; and shoot wild fowl. The 1621 harvest was successful, with a fine supply of maize, barley and other foods (although the pea crop failed). This was the occasion for the famous harvest festival that became the mythic "First Thanksgiving." The arrival of 35 new settlers on the Fortune in November 1621 put an unexpected strain on supplies, and the less successful harvest of 1622 led to straitened circumstances until the autumn of 1623. After that, Gov. William Bradford noted in *Of Plimoth Plantation* that "any general want or famine hath not been amongst them to this day."

By 1627 (chosen as the date for Plimoth Plantation's reconstruction because it is the most fully documented year in the colony's first decade), each of the thirty-plus households had its own garden plot, and each resident—man, woman or child—had an acre in the fields. The population had exceeded 150. The primary field crop was maize, although traditional English crops were grown as well. We are not sure that plowing was possible at this point, but we assume it was. There were 16 cattle in 1627, of which 5 were producing milk. There were also at least 20 she-goats, and the combined milk production of these animals provided the colony with a fair amount of "white meats," as dairy products were called. There were a few sheep, while swine and chickens were considered too numerous to list. The forest and seashore provided wild game and shellfish. Ducks, geese, cranes, small birds, rabbits, turkeys, quail, grouse, eels, lobsters, mussels, clams and winkles were all eaten. Deer were beyond the colonists' ability to bring down, but they often acquired venison from the skilled Indian hunters. Fishing was done with a number of small boats, or shallops.

In 1627 the colony depended on supplies from England for many of its needs. (Tools, equipment and most clothing came from London, for the village could not support many craftsmen.) But it was as self-sufficient as most English villages in the matter of food: Husbandmen fed themselves but bought manufactured items and supplies such as salt, spices, dried fruit and sugar that they could neither make nor raise. Since ships arrived regularly, supplies such as malt were probably available as predictably as they were in England.

Basic food supplies were another matter, at least initially. Governor Bradford stated in 1621 that the Merchant Adventurers, the group of London speculators that financed the colony and sent supplies, never supported the settlers "with any supply of victuals more afterwards . . . for all the [victuals] the company sent at any time was always too short for those people who came with it." The colony was obliged to buy foodstuffs such as peas from the English fishermen who came in fleets every spring, or corn and beans from the Indians in the early years. By 1627 the colonists had become largely self-sufficient.

The cultural context of cooking and eating is paramount in presenting an accurate picture of Pilgrim life, and the change in seasons may be the most important factor of all. The Plantation has divided its cooking and preservation program into segments spanning its visitor season, which annually runs from April through November.

The year begins with spring (April 1 to mid-May): the planting of fields and gardens, the salting of cod and alewives and a diet largely based on food preserved from the previous growing season. Shellfish, wild fowl and rabbits are among the few fresh items. Some milking is done toward the end of the period, as is brewing of beer. There are still sufficient grains and legumes for breads and pottage.

Early summer (mid-May to midsummer) sees the depletion of the preserved stores of salt meat, pickles and grains except for maize. It is a period of privation in the village. The winter foods run low before much has come up in the fields or gardens to replace them. There is a heavy reliance on white meats and fish, as the wild fowl have departed and the rabbits have got wormy. Some of the young males among the sheep and goats end up on the spit and in the pot. There is never any beef, since the herd must be expanded for milk cows and oxen.

Toward late summer (midsummer to mid-August) the gardens begin to produce herbs, as vegetables were called. Little meat or beer is as yet available, but there are more fresh things to add to the fish and white meats. Cornbread is the only bread made, except for on special occasions, until the grain harvest. Seeds from the garden plants are also collected for the next season.

Harvest (mid-August to early October) brings the annual period of abundance. The grain stores are in and being flailed. At the end of the period the maize is harvested, and a harvest celebration follows. Vegetables, wild fruit, berries and nuts are all plentiful. Beer is brewed from the newly malted barley, and the beginning of the slaughtering brings fresh meat.

The winter period (mid-October through November) follows. The village is full of fish and swine being salted and smoked. The gardens are made ready for winter, roots are put down and herbs are dried as the village closes in for the long, cold season ahead.

As for the famous first harvest festival of 1621, now known as the "First Thanksgiving," we have no exact bill of fare. The event is mentioned in only two passages, one in William Bradford's *Of Plimoth Plantation* and the other in a letter by colonist Edward Winslow to a friend in England. We do not know a specific date for the three-day celebration, but it was between September 21, when the Mayflower's shallop returned from Massachusetts Bay, and November 9, when the Fortune arrived with new settlers.

From the two passages, we learn that the feast included cod, sea bass, wild fowl (such as turkeys, ducks, geese and swans), cornmeal (and probably wheat), and five deer brought by the Indians. Meat, fish and bread were the most important elements of the English diet at this time, although fruits and "herbs" were also eaten.

Dishes were not prepared with the intent of allowing each guest a portion. As at a modern potluck dinner, each dish provided only a limited amount of food. Courses didn't proceed from soups to sweets, but tended to contain all sort of foods at the same time. The table was set with a variety of dishes, and they were passed or fetched by the children and servants, who waited on their own families.

The meats were roasted or boiled in traditional English fashion, and the fish were boiled or perhaps grilled after the Indian fashion. It is quite possible that shellfish were not a feature at the feast. Although they were plentiful and formed a large part of the Pilgrims' diet in the early years, they were looked on as poverty fare and hence not appropriate at a feast. Breads were skillet breads cooked by the fire, or perhaps risen breads baked in a clay or loam oven. The "herbs" were either boiled along with the meats as "sauce," or used in "sallets." Native fruits, such as raspberries, wild cherries, wild strawberries, and blueberries, were no longer in season at harvest time, but they were often dried by the Indians and may have been preserved by the colonists as well.

The term "vegetables" was not in use at this time; edible plants were known as sallet herbs, potherbs or roots. A sallet was a vegetable dish either cooked or raw, and either "simple" or "compound"—that is, made from one ingredient or a mixture. Sallet or vegetable dishes were not greatly popular at this time; therefore they are not always mentioned, although they were served fairly frequently.

To get an even clearer picture of the first harvest feast, think about the familiar items that most likely were *not* on the table. Apple, pear and other fruit trees not native to New England would not have borne fruit for years after planting; therefore there was no cider at the first harvest festival. Potatoes were known to botanists, and sweet potatoes enjoyed a mild popularity in England among the well-to-do, but they were not available in early New England. The corn grown by the Pilgrims and local Indians was a flint variety; they did not have sweet corn on the cob, or popcorn. There was no Indian pudding in its modern form because there was no molasses. Cranberries may have been used in "puddings in the belly" (stuffings), but not in their familiar forms as jelly or preserves, because sugar was scarce. Celery was unknown. Olives were imported into England, but it is quite unlikely that they came to Plymouth in 1620. (Edward Winslow wrote home that "sallet oil," or olive oil, would be a good thing to bring on future voyages.) Even creamed onions would not have been possible; although onions and milk may have been available, there were no flour-thickened sauces or gravies in 1621. (Bread crumbs or egg yolks were used as thickeners.) Tea and coffee were not in use in England, nor known to the Pilgrims.

The 50 Pilgrims and 90 Indians who attended the dinner sat at cloth-covered tables on benches and forms, with a few chairs for the more important men. The participants ate with knives and a few spoons, but no forks. Large linen napkins, about 3-feet square, were necessary, since hands were used both to serve and to eat. Trenchers—small square or round wooden plates—were used, sometimes shared by two people. Pottages, or soups, were eaten from bowls. There would have been no table decorations in the modern sense, for decorated salts and elaborate food sculptures were not a part of the yeoman tradition familiar to the Pilgrims.

Food production and preparation at Plimoth Plantation today rely on the materials cited above, but this is only part of the story. Just as important is the cultural factor: English yeoman taste.

The 1627 Plymouth planters were mostly of the yeoman level (upper-middle status) of English society. Only a few might have aspired to the lower gentry, and a slightly larger number had been common laborers. The majority were neither poor nor socially isolated except in the matter of the Separatist faith. They were familiar with an agricultural existence, and they were probably among the more ambitious and adventuresome of their contemporaries.

Early accounts go into great detail about what these people found to eat in the New World. Writing before 1654, Edward Johnson noted:

You have heard in what extream penury these people were in at first. . . . But now take notice how the right hand of the Most High hath altered all, and men of mean rank are urging [other colonists] to buy bread of them and now good white and wheaten bread is not dainty, but even ordinary man hath his choice . . . beside flesh is now no rare food, beef, pork, and mutton being frequent in many houses, so that this poor *wilderness hath not onely equalized England in food but goes beyond it in some places for the great plenty of wine and sugar, which is ordinarily spent, apples, pears and quince tarts instead of their former Pumpkin Pies, Poultry they have plenty, and great rarity, and in their feasts have not forgotten the English fashion of stirring up their appetites with variety of cooking their food.*

A number of sources contain long lists of available foodstuffs, but they seldom tell how these were prepared. We must look back to England for the taste of the middling sort of Englishman. This can be found in a number of cookbooks aimed at the housewives of the lower gentry and prosperous yeomen. The most popular was Gervase Markham's *Countrey Contentments of the English Huswife* (1623), but there are earlier ones such as Thomas Dawson's *The Good Huswifes Jewell* (1587), *The Good Huswifes Handmaide for the Kitchin* (1594) and John Murrell's *A Book of Cookerie* (1612). All represent the same sort of cuisine, and the authors credit housewives with providing some of the recipes. The range of the recipes goes from the elaborate high medieval style to fairly simple dishes.

It has been suggested that there were two parallel English cuisines at this time. One was a court cuisine consisting of dishes beloved of early food historians, who used these recipes to indicate the amusingly benighted taste of our ancestors. The other was a simple subsistence fare that lacked the flamboyance of the court cuisine and that remarkably resembled the taste of our own present-day country cooks. This may be a misreading of the record. It is more likely that the medieval taste exhibited in the "huswife" cookbooks represents the solid middle of seventeenth-century taste, with the extremes being the elaborate dishes of the rich and the horse bread (made of ground peas, beans, and tares primarily as feed for horses) and roots of the poor. It was, however, one cuisine.

A number of authorities note the shift toward simpler foods, and some put it down to the Puritan influence. How the Puritans were able to cause the demise of medieval cuisine during the Restoration is unclear. The English Puritans had little trouble with large dinners. Feasting was one of the few enjoyments and celebrations they could countenance.

Since the Pilgrims were among the more literate and aware citizens of their time, both as Puritans and as people who left their places of origin to go to Holland, London and, of course, the New

World, they had been exposed to culinary fashions. One might conclude that their Puritan beliefs would have cut them off from an interest in good cooking, but there is no evidence that this is so. In fact, they had a lively enthusiasm for the foodstuffs of their new home, and as long as gluttony or drunkenness did not result, they seemed to approve of both good food and drink whenever possible.

This is not to say that the Pilgrims or their contemporaries always ate the sort of dishes found in the cookbooks, any more than we always eat under the aegis of Julia Child. Some could afford it only at times, and even prosperous people probably ate many simple and unimaginitive meals, just as their counterparts do today in the "meat and potatoes" syndrome. It is not economics, but comfortable familiarity that dictates such a choice. In the seventeenth century, a large proportion of simple meals need not indicate that nothing else was appreciated or available. It was the Pilgrims' *conception* of what constituted good food that was quite different from the belief in natural simplicity that emerged in the eighteenth century.

The foodways program at Plimoth Plantation must communicate the reality of medieval taste and demonstrate the cultural difference between 1627 Plymouth and modern America. While most village cooking remains at the poor end of the spectrum, the wealthier families attempt to replicate the yeoman cuisine of their peers back in the old country. The village food thus represents the fading vestige of the old medieval order in the New World.

The Plantation presents the preparation and consumption of food as traditionally as possible in the historic area, but for twentieth-century pragmatic reasons a considerable backup program is necessary as well. We are obliged to buy stores the Pilgrims acquired from the sea, woods and fields. Fish and shellfish, except for alewives and mussels, must be bought. The time when enormous lobsters could be found for the taking in the shallow waters of Plymouth Harbor is gone forever.

Some meats that we raise at present must be supplemented with market supplies, such as chicken and pork. Our ducks and rabbits also come from a supermarket rather than the local thicket, but we have a behind-the-scenes program to raise game animals to supply the village in the autumn. Canada geese, wild turkeys and quail are being raised, and we hope to add ducks, cottontail rabbits and other local species in time.

Since we do not have the acreage of the original settlement's fields, we must buy our cereals both in grain and on the ground so that we can bring in a "harvest" to the village in proper fashion. Our token fields are planted with maize, meslin (wheat and rye together) and peas, or are left fallow. The most noticeable food sources in the village itself, barring the livestock, are the garden plots kept by each household. These gardens are mucked and planted in the spring, and they furnish the necessary "herbs" for cooking and storage throughout the season. The gardens were laid out in raised beds in period fashion and contain plants mentioned in early sources.

It has become our aim at Plimoth Plantation to show visitors that the Pilgrims were not just like ourselves in funny clothes, but that they inhabited a society as unlike ours in many ways as many in the world today. Their tastes and values are not ours clouded by incapacity, but a quite different set that are more closely related to those in the Classical world than they are to today's. Their vanished cuisine graphically represents an important part of this unfamiliar world picture. It is vital to our understanding of the Pilgrims that their cuisine be exhibited in all its authentic glory.

III

Seventeenth-Century Recipes for the Twentieth-Century Cook

BY THE STAFF OF PLIMOTH PLANTATION

A CHEWET PIE

Take the brawnes and wings of Capons and Chickens after they have been rosted, and pull away the skin; then shred them with fine Mutton suet very small; then season it with cloves, mace, cinamon, sugar and salt, then put to raysins of the Sunne and currants, and slic't dates, and orange pills, and being well mixt together, put it into small coffins made for the purpose, and strow on top of them good store of caraway Comfets: then cover them, and bake them with a gentle heate and these Chewets you may also make rosted Veale, seasoned as before shewed, and of all parts the loyne is the best. (Gervase Markham, Country Contentments, 1623)

Chewets were small pies similar in size to modern English pork pies. They were made with a variety of fillings; chicken, oysters and beef are all mentioned in the cookbooks of the day. The mixture of finely chopped meat with dried fruits and spices is similar to mincemeat, although it is not aged. Completely sealed by the pastry, chewet pies are easy to pack and carry for lunches or picnics.

Caraway comfets are candied caraway seeds, available at Near Eastern food shops.

Preparation time: about 1 hour

1. Preheat the oven to 350 degrees.
2. In a large bowl, mix together the chicken, suet, currants, dates, raisins, mace, cinnamon, cloves, orange rind, sugar and salt. Toss the ingredients to blend them thoroughly.

4 cups coarsely chopped cooked chicken
1 cup finely chopped suet
1/4 cup dried currants
1/4 cup chopped pitted dates
1/2 cup seedless raisins
1/2 teaspoon mace
1/2 teaspoon cinnamon
1/4 teaspoon ground cloves
1 1/2 teaspoons grated orange rind
2 tablespoons sugar
1 1/2 teaspoons salt

3. Roll out a little more than half the dough, and place it in the bottom of a 9-inch pie plate. Fill the pie with the chicken mixture. Sprinkle the caraway seeds over the filling, and dot the top with butter. Roll out the remaining pastry, and cover the pie with a top crust. Trim the edges, and crimp them to seal them. Cut slits in the top crust to vent the steam.
4. Bake the pie for 40 minutes, or until the top crust is nicely brown.

1 recipe Flaky Pie Pastry (see p. 183)
1/2 teaspoon candied caraway seeds (available at Near Eastern food shops)
1/4 cup unsalted butter

Makes 1 (9-inch) pie

PEASE POTTAGE

R
286

To boyle yong peason or Beanes. Firste shale them and seethe them in faire water, then take them out of the water and put them into boyling milk, then take the yolks of Egs with crums of bread, and ginger, and straine them through a strainer with the said milk, then take chopped percely, Saffron and Salt, and serve it forth for Pottage. (A. W., A Book of Cookrye, 1591)

Pease pottage or porridge, well known today through the old nursery rhyme if not through personal experience, was a staple dish in the seventeenth century. This recipe is for a spruced-up version of the standard pease pottage, for it calls for green peas or beans, the *green* indicating unripeness rather than color (unripe corn was likewise called green corn). Made with "green" peas rather than dried ones, this is a more elegant soup than the common thick pottage.

Preparation time: about 1¼ hours

5 pounds fresh peas, shelled (about 4 cups)

1. Place the shelled peas in a large saucepan, and cover them with water. Bring the water to a boil, then reduce the heat and simmer until the peas are soft, about 15 minutes. Drain the peas, and set them aside.

2 cups milk
2 egg yolks, beaten
⅔ cup dry bread crumbs, preferably homemade
¼ teaspoon ground ginger

2. In a 2- to 3-quart saucepan, heat the milk to just under a boil. Add the cooked peas, beaten egg yolks, bread crumbs and ginger. Stir to mix the ingredients. Transfer the mixture in batches to a food mill or food processor fitted with a steel knife, and puree until the mixture is smooth. Return the puree to the saucepan, and thoroughly reheat it.

½ cup minced parsley
Pinch of saffron (optional)
Salt to taste

3. Add the parsley, saffron (if desired) and salt. Stir to mix, and serve the pottage immediately.

Serves 4 to 6 as a main course, 8 as a first course

SEVENTEENTH-CENTURY BREAD

R 2862

Bread was one of the staple foods of the seventeenth century; consumption averaged 1 pound a day. The quality of the bread was determined by the type and fineness of the flour, ranging from the well-ground and sifted white all-wheat flour to mixes of flour and bran to coarse meal. In times of famine, bread was made from crushed peas or beans. The English government regulated the size and quality of loaves of bakers' bread, which changed from year to year in response to the grain harvest.

Bread was made in large quantities, with flour measured by the bushel. Dough was mixed in large troughs and kneaded with a brake, a baker's kneading machine, or wrapped in cloth and kneaded with the feet. The rising agent was "barm," the yeast created when beer was brewed. Quantities have been reduced in this recipe to make a manageable piece of dough, and the recipe has been adapted for modern yeast.

Preparation time: about 4 hours

1 C. water, if using breadmachine

1. Stir the sugar into ~~the water~~. Sprinkle in the yeast. Let the mixture sit until the yeast bubbles to the surface. Stir in the white and whole-wheat flours. Mix well. Cover the batter with waxed paper and a towel. Let it sit until it is bubbly, 30 minutes to 1 hour.

1 tablespoon sugar
2 cups warm water *(1½ cups) in b/m*
1 tablespoon active dry yeast
1½ cups white flour
½ cup whole-wheat flour

2. Stir down the batter, and add the salt, the rye flour and the corn flour.

1 teaspoon salt
½ cup rye flour
1 cup corn flour (2 tarspns)

3. Spread the whole-wheat flour over a work surface, and turn the dough onto it. Knead the wheat flour into the dough, sprinkling with more white flour if the dough is still too sticky. Knead until the dough is firm but springy.

½ cup whole-wheat flour

4. Grease a clean bowl with the vegetable oil. Set the dough in the bowl, and turn the dough over to coat it completely with the oil. Cover the dough with waxed paper and a towel, and set it to rise until it is double in bulk, about 1 hour, or overnight in the refrigerator.

1 tablespoon vegetable oil (omit)

5. Preheat the oven to 375 degrees.

6. Punch down the dough, and divide it in two. Knead it into two round loaves. With a sharp knife, cut a slash around the circumference of each loaf, and prick the top. Set the loaves on a lightly floured cookie sheet. The dough need not rise again before baking.

7. Bake the bread for 45 minutes, or until a tap on the bottom of a loaf produces a hollow sound. Set the loaves on racks to cool.

Makes 2 round loaves

MINC'T PIE

Take a Leg of Mutton, and cut of the best flesh from the bone, and parboyle it well: then put to it three pound of the best Mutton suet, and shred it very small; then spred it abroad, and season it with pepper and salt, cloves and mace: then put in good store of currants, great raysons and prunes cleane washt and pickt, a few dates slic't, and some orange pills slic't: then being all well mixt together, put it into a coffin, or into divers coffins, and so bake them: and when they are served up open the liddes, and strow store of suger on the top of the meate, and upon the lid. And in this sort you may also bake Beefe or Veale; onely the Beefe would not be parboyled, and the Veale will aske a double quantitie of suet. (Gervase Markham, Countrey Contentments, 1623)

Minced pies—meat pies flavored with dried fruit and spices finely chopped together—were quite popular in the seventeenth century, though not with everyone. The extreme Puritan protesters against the Church of England found in the Christmas minced pie a symbol of the worldly luxury and religious superstition they detested. They decried minced pies as a satanic snare for the unwary. But there is no indication that the Pilgrims, good Calvinists though they were, had any particular animus against the inoffensive minced pie. Certainly the minced pie in time became a traditional part of the Thanksgiving holiday, until Christmas returned to reclaim its own in the middle of the nineteenth century (Christmas was not celebrated in Massachusetts until 1840). The pie is also a very good illustration of seventeenth-century taste in cookery, with its spices, dried fruits and admixture of meat with many other ingredients.

Preparation time: about 1 1/2 hours

1. Cut the meat into 1-inch chunks. Place the meat in a large saucepan, and cover it with water. Bring the water to a boil. Reduce the heat to medium, and continue to cook the meat, covered, for 10 to 15 minutes, until the meat is cooked through but still tender. Remove the meat, and allow it to cool.

2. Place the chunks of meat and the suet in a food processor fitted with a steel blade. Pulsate the machine on and off until the meat and suet are coarsely chopped. (Or chop the meat by hand, or grind it coarsely in a meat grinder.) Transfer the mixture from the processor bowl to a large mixing bowl, and add the prunes, dates, raisins, currants, orange peel, mace, cloves, salt and pepper. Mix well until all ingredients are evenly distributed.

3. Preheat the oven to 350 degrees.

4. Line a 9-inch pie pan with a little more than half the pastry, and trim the edge. Fill the pastry with the mincemeat mixture. Cover with a second layer of pastry, trim the edge, and crimp to seal. Make a few cuts in the top crust to vent the steam. Bake the pie for about 40 minutes, or until the crust is brown. Serve the pie sprinkled with sugar, if desired.

Makes 1 (9-inch) pie

1 pound lamb meat, from the shoulder or the thickest part of a leg

1/2 pound suet, cut in small pieces
2/3 cup chopped pitted prunes
1/3 cup chopped pitted dates
1/4 cup seedless raisins
1/3 cup dried currants
1/4 cup chopped orange peel
1/2 teaspoon ground mace
1/4 teaspoon ground cloves
Salt and freshly ground black pepper to taste

1 recipe Flaky Pie Pastry (see page 183)
Sugar (optional)

BOILED SMALL FISH

To boyle small Fish, as Roches, Daces, Gudgeon or Flounders, boyle White-wine and water together with a bunch of choise Hearbs, and a little whole Mace: when all is boyled wel together, put in your fish, and skum it well: then put in the soale of a Manchet, a good quantitie of sweet Butter, and season it with Pepper and Veriuyce, and so serve it in upon Sippets, and adorne the sides of the dish with Sugar. (Gervase Markham, Countrey Contentments, 1623)

Fish was a very popular part of the seventeenth-century English diet. For those who lived inland, however, fresh fish was something of a luxury. Without refrigeration, the fish had to be preserved by smoking or salting. Freshwater fish could be caught in small streams, and some colonists ensured their supply by building small freshwater ponds where such fish as roach and tench could be kept until needed.

Preparation time: about 25 minutes

1 cup water
1 cup white wine
2 teaspoons thyme
2 teaspoons savory
2 teaspoons marjoram
2 teaspoons rosemary
2 teaspoons minced parsley
1 teaspoon ground mace

1. In a 2- to 3-quart saucepan, mix the water, wine, thyme, savory, marjoram, rosemary, parsley and mace. Bring the mixture to a boil.

2 pounds smelts or small
  mackerel, cleaned

2. Add the fish to the pot. Simmer them 5 to 15 minutes, until they are done. Remove the fish from the pot, and keep them warm.

Crusts from 2 slices bread
1/4 cup unsalted butter
2 tablespoons cider vinegar
Freshly ground black pepper
  to taste

3. Add the bread crusts, butter, vinegar and pepper to the broth. Simmer a few minutes, until the bread crusts have disintegrated. Serve the broth over the fish.

Serves 6

TO MAKE A CUSTARD

Break your egges into a bowle, and put your Creame into an other bowle and streine your egges into the creame, and put saffron, cloves and mace, and a litle synamon and ginger, and if you will, some suger and butter, and season it with salt, and melt your butter, and stirre it with the ladle a good while, and dubbe your Custard with dates or currants. (Thomas Dawson, The Good Huswifes Jewell, 1587)

Large dishes of custard were usually included in feasts of the seventeenth century. In *Dining With William Shakespeare*, Madge Lorwin notes that it was considered highly amusing at these feasts for a fool, fully dressed, to leap over the heads of the guests and land in the custard, spattering everyone nearby. This entertainment was similar in nature to the practice of putting live animals and birds into pie shells, to fly, jump or slither toward the guests once the pie was cut. The "four-and-twenty blackbirds baked in a pie" might well have been served next to the custard.

Preparation time: about 45 minutes, plus cooling

1. In a medium bowl, whisk together the egg yolks, cloves, mace, cinnamon, ginger, sugar and salt. Set the mixture aside.

4 egg yolks
¹/₂ teaspoon ground cloves
¹/₂ teaspoon ground mace
¹/₂ teaspoon cinnamon
¹/₂ teaspoon ground ginger
¹/₂ cup sugar
Pinch salt

2. In the top of a double boiler, over boiling water, scald the cream with the butter.

4 cups heavy cream
2 tablespoons unsalted butter

3. Slowly pour the scalded cream into the egg yolk mixture, whisking continuously. Return the entire mixture to the double boiler and cook it, stirring frequently, until the custard thickens.

4. Pour the mixture into the serving bowl, and let it cool. Refrigerate it until serving time.

½ cup dates, pitted and
   sliced
½ cup dried currants

5. Just before serving, decorate the top of the custard with the dates and currants.

Serves 4 to 6

TO FRIE CHICKINS

Take your Chickins and let them boyle in verie good sweete broath a pretie while, and take the Chickens out, & quarter them out in peeces, and put them into a Frying pan with sweet Butter, and let them stewe in the pan, but you must not let them be browne with frying, and then put out the butter out of the pan, and then take a little sweete broath and as much Vergice, and the yolkes of two Egges, and beat them together, and put in a litle Nutmegges, Synamom and Ginger, and Pepper into the sauce, and then put them all into the pan to the Chickens, and stirre them together in the pan, and put them into a dish and serve them up. (Thomas Dawson, *The Good Huswifes Jewell*, 1587)

Chickens were the earliest domesticated animals in Plymouth Colony. In the spring of 1623, Edward Winslow found the sachem (Wampanoag hereditary leader) Massasoit severely ill and close to death. Winslow sent a messenger back to Plymouth for some chickens to make a broth, but in the meantime he made a soup of cornmeal, wild fowl, sassafras root and strawberry leaves, to good effect. When the chickens arrived, Massasoit chose not to kill them, but to keep them to breed.

Preparation time: about 25 minutes

2 tablespoons unsalted
   butter
2 skinless, boneless chicken
   breasts (about 10
   ounces), halved
1 cup chicken stock,
   preferably homemade

1. In a large skillet, preferably nonstick, melt the butter. When it begins to foam, place the chicken breasts in the skillet. Sauté them on one side just until the surface turns opaque; then turn them and sauté them on the other side. Add the chicken stock, and, over medium-high heat, poach the chicken breasts, covered, about 10 to 15 minutes, until the juices no longer run pink when the thickest part of a breast is pierced with a fork. Remove the meat to a heated platter, and keep it warm in the oven.

2. To the stock in which the chicken was poached, add the wine, nutmeg, cinnamon and ginger. Stir to mix well. Over high heat, reduce the liquid by about one-third. Remove the pan from the heat. Spoon about ¼ cup of the liquid into the egg yolks, and whisk to blend. Pour the egg yolk mixture into the liquid, and whisk to blend, gently warming the sauce over a very low heat. Do not allow the egg yolks to curdle. Add the salt and pepper.

3. Remove the platter from the oven, and pour the sauce over the chicken breasts. Serve them immediately.

Serves 4

¼ *cup white wine or lemon juice*
¼ *teaspoon freshly grated nutmeg*
¼ *teaspoon cinnamon*
¼ *teaspoon ground ginger*
4 *egg yolks, well beaten*
Salt and freshly ground black pepper to taste

TO BOILE ONIONS

Take a good many onions and cut them in four quarters, set them on the fire in as much water as you think will boyle them tender, and when they be clean skimmed, put in a good many of small raisons, halfe a spooneful of grose pepper, a good peece of Sugar, and a little Salte, and when the onions be through boiled, beat the yolk of an Egge with Vergious, and put into your pot and so serve it upon soppes. If you will poch, Egges and lay upon them. (Thomas Dawson, *The Second Part of the Good Huswifes Jewell,* 1597)

After being quite unfashionable, vegetables were just returning to popularity in the early seventeenth century. The wealthy in early Tudor England preferred to eat as much meat, fowl and fish as possible, washed down with wine or beer. Except as flavorings for stews and other meat dishes, vegetables had been considered indications of a common or peasant diet. Vegetable dishes or "sallets" were still seldom found on the tables of conservative folk who could afford to indulge the English taste for meat. Onions were among the few vegetables (including artichokes and asparagus) considered good enough to be cooked as a separate dish.

In Pilgrim times the word *vegetable* had not yet been introduced into common parlance, and edible plants were all referred to as herbs, from "potherbs," such as beets, carrots, marigolds, parsley and strawberries, to "sallet herbs" and roots such as onions, beans, artichokes, purslane and horseradish. The plants now considered herbs were classified either as sweet herbs (basil, marjoram, sage and thyme) or physic herbs (Angelica, feverfew, rue, southernwood and garlic). When the colonists had herb gardens, they were not limited to the last two categories, as they would be today, but included vegetables as well.

Preparation time: about 50 minutes

About 2 1/2 pounds medium onions
5 cups water
1 cup dried currants
1 teaspoon whole peppercorns
2 tablespoons sugar
1 teaspoon salt

1. Peel and quarter the onions. Place them in a saucepan, and cover them with the water. Bring the water to a boil, skimming off any froth. Add the currants, peppercorns, sugar and salt. Lower the heat, and simmer 1/2 hour.

4 egg yolks
3 tablespoons cider vinegar

2. Beat the egg yolks with the vinegar. Slowly beat in 1/2 cup of the onion broth. Drain the onions, discarding the rest of the broth, and stir in the egg mixture.

8 slices toast or 8 poached eggs

3. Serve the onions over slices of toast or with poached eggs.

Serves 4

STEWED JERUSALEM ARTICHOKES

These rootes [jerusalem artichokes] are dressed divers waies; some boil them in water and after stew them with sacke and butter, adding a little Ginger: others bake them in pies putting Marrow, Dates, Ginger, Raisons of the Sun, Sack, &c. Others some other way, as they are led by their skill in Cookerie. (John Gerard, *The Herball or General Historie of Plants*, 1597)

The jerusalem artichoke, a 6- to 8-foot sunflower native to southeast Massachusetts, was once cultivated by the Wampanoag Indians for its edible tubers. These tubers, now sold in supermarkets as "sun chokes," were thought to resemble in taste and texture the globe artichoke, which was popular in the seventeenth century. They enjoyed a brief period of novelty when they were introduced into England about 1600. Like the groundnut, the tubers of the jerusalem artichoke were a welcome food source during the periods of dearth suffered during the first years of the American colonies.

The name of the plant, which the herbalist John Gerard asserted is an illustration that "those who vulgarly impose names upon plants have little either judgment or knowledge of them," comes from the plant's Italian name, *Girasole articiocco* (sunflower artichoke). *Girasole* was quickly corrupted to Jerusalem, and the plant's English name was born.

Preparation time: about 30 minutes

1. Scrub the jerusalem artichokes and cut them into halves, or thirds if they are large. Place them in a 2-quart saucepan, and barely cover them with water. Heat the water to boiling; then reduce the heat and simmer 10 minutes, until the jerusalem artichokes are fork-tender. Drain them.

2. Mash the jerusalem artichokes. Add the butter, sherry and ginger. Reheat briefly over low to medium heat.

2 pounds jerusalem artichokes (sun chokes)

4 tablespoons unsalted butter
¼ cup medium-dry sherry
½ teaspoon ground ginger

Serves 6 to 8

JERUSALEM ARTICHOKE PIE

Preparation time: about 1¼ hours

1. Sift together the whole-wheat and white flours with the salt into a large mixing bowl. Cut in the butter with two knives or a pastry blender until the mixture has the texture of coarse meal. Add just enough ice water to form an adhesive dough.

2. Divide the dough in two pieces, one slightly larger than the other. Roll out each piece to a thickness of about ⅛ inch. Line a 9-inch pie plate with the larger piece, and trim the edge. Reserve the remaining dough for the top crust.

3. Preheat the oven to 350 degrees.

1 cup whole-wheat flour
1 cup white flour
⅛ teaspoon salt
½ cup unsalted butter, well chilled
¼ cup ice water

1 pound jerusalem
   artichokes, peeled and
   thinly sliced
2 tablespoons unsalted
   butter
¹/₄ cup seedless raisins
¹/₄ cup chopped dates
¹/₄ teaspoon minced fresh
   gingerroot
2 tablespoons medium-dry
   sherry
¹/₂ cup sugar

4. Layer the jerusalem artichoke slices in the pie pan, and dot them with the butter. Add the raisins, dates, ginger, sherry and sugar, sprinkling them evenly over the artichokes. Cover the pie with the top crust, trim it and crimp the edges to seal them.

5. Bake the pie for 45 minutes to 1 hour, or until the top crust is nicely brown.

Makes 1 (9-inch) pie

SAUCE FOR A HEN OR A PULLET

To make sauce for an old Hen or Pullet, take a good quantitie of beere and salt, and mixe them well together with a few fine breadcrummes, and boil them on a chafing-dish and coales, then take the yelks or three or fowre hard Eggs, and being shred small, put it to the Beere, and boile it also: then the Hen being almost enough, take three or fowre spoonefull of the gravie which comes from her and put it to also, and boil altogether to an indeifferent thickenesse: which done, suffer it to boile no more, but only keepe it warm on the fire, and put into it the iuyce of two or three Orenges, & the slices of Lemmon pills shred small, and the slices of Orenges also having the upper rine taken away: then the Henne beeing broken up, take the brawnes thereof, and shredding them small, put it into the sauce also; and stirring all well together, put it hot into a cleane warme dish, and lay the Henne (broke up) in the same. (Gervase Markham, *Countrey Contentments,* 1623)

This sauce was as good for that staple of the English farm table, the old hen that had passed her egg-laying days, as it was for a young pullet. In this period sauces were thickened with fine bread crumbs, as flour-based roux were unknown until the end of the seventeenth century.

The combination of sour beer and tart citrus was a favorite in Pilgrim times. Lemons and oranges were imported into England and even America in this period. Edward Winslow urged later immigrants to bring lemons with them on their voyages—as the Massachusetts colonists did, according to Governor Winthrop.

Preparation time: about 40 minutes

1. In a saucepan, boil together the ale, bread crumbs and salt. Crumble the egg yolks, and add them to the ale mixture. Add the butter, and boil all together for 5 minutes. Reduce the heat to a simmer.

2 cups English ale
¹/₂ cup dry, coarse bread crumbs, preferably homemade
2 teaspoons salt
Yolks of 4 hard-boiled eggs
2 tablespoons unsalted butter

2. Add the orange juice, lemon rind and orange slices to the mixture. Continue to simmer it. If the mixture is too thick, thin it with a little more beer or orange juice.

³/₄ cup strained fresh orange juice
1 tablespoon grated lemon rind
1 orange, peeled and sliced

3. Stir the chicken meat into the sauce, and continue simmering until the meat is heated through. Serve immediately.

6 cups chopped cooked chicken

Serves 6 to 8

A GRAND SALLET

The youngest and smallest leaves of spinage, the smallest also of sorrel, well washed currans, and red beets round the center being finely carved, oyl and vinegar, and the dish garnished with lemon and beets. (Robert May, The Accomplisht Cook, *1671)*

Many of the seventeenth-century salads and vegetable dishes we know are found only in the cookbooks of the wealthy, for cookbooks for the middle class contain only a few "sallet" dishes. "Sallets" included any vegetable dish, cooked or raw. They were usually divided into simple sallets, which consisted of a single "herb" (vegetable), and compound sallets, which contained several ingredients. A boiled compound sallet, for example, might include carrots, beets, purslane and turnips.

In the 1650s, Gov. William Bradford found the following "herbs," destined for use in sallets and stews, in Plymouth gardens:

> All sorts of roots and herbs in gardens grow,
> Parsnips, carrots, turnips, or what you'll sow,
> Onions, melons, cucumbers, radishes,
> Skirets, beets, coleworts, and fair cabbages.
> (*Bradford's Letter Book*, 1794)

(Purslane is a prostrate succulent, now considered a weed. Skirret is a parsnip-like vegetable whose roots grow in bunches. Coleworts are the members of the cabbage family, such as kale, broccoli and cauliflower.)

This recipe is a good example of a raw compound sallet with a cooked ingredient.

Preparation time: about 30 minutes

8 small beets

1. Trim and scrub the beets. Place them in a 1-quart saucepan with water to cover. Bring the water to a boil, lower the heat to a simmer, and cook the beets until they are tender, about 15 minutes. Drain and peel the beets, and cut into thin slices.

1/2 pound fresh spinach
1/4 pound sorrel

2. While the beets are cooking, wash and pick over the spinach and sorrel leaves, shake them dry and mix them together in a medium salad bowl.

2/3 cup dried currants

3. Add the currants and the slices from six beets to the greens, and mix well.

6 tablespoons olive oil
6 tablespoons red wine
    vinegar

4. Mix the oil and vinegar well, pour it over the salad and toss the salad to mix it.

1 lemon, seeded and thinly
    sliced

5. Garnish the salad with the remaining two sliced beets and the sliced lemon.

Serves 6 to 8

ANOTHER COMPOUND SALLAT

To compound an excellent Sallat, and which indeed is usuall at great feasts, and upon Princes tables: Take a good quantitie of blancht Almonds, and with your shredding Knife cut them grossly; then take as many Raisins of the Sunne cleane washt, and the stones pickt out, as many Figs shred like the Almonds, as many Capers, twice so many Olyves, and as many Currants as of all the rest cleane washt: a good handfull of the small tender leaves of red Sage and Spinage: mixe all these well together with good store of Sugar, and lay them in the bottome of a great dish; then put unto them Vinegar and Oyle, and scrape more Sugar over all: then take Orenges and Lemons, and paring away the outward pills, cut them into thinne slices, then with those slices cover the Sallet al over; which done, take the fine thinne leave of the red Coleflower, and with them cover the Orenges and Lemons all over; then over those red leaves lay another course of old Olives, and the slices of well pickled Cucumbers, together with the very inward Heart of your Cabbage lettice cut into slices; then adorne the sides of the dish, and the top of the Sallet with mo slices of Lemons and Orenges and so serve it up. (Gervase Markham, *Countrey Contentments*, 1623)

Salads gained in popularity as the seventeenth century progressed. Although vegetables were still considered inferior to meat in the cuisine of the day, they had their place in the nutritional theory of the period. The line between herbs as medicine and "herbs" (or vegetables) as foods was not a strict one; a plant might be both at the same time. In creating a proper sallet, it was necessary to balance the humoral (nutritional *and* medicinal) qualities of one herb with another. All foods were thought to be either hot or cold, wet or dry in their effect on the human body. For example, if one ate too many cold, moist foods such as lettuce or melons, they might cause illness. Good dietary practice required that they be offset by hot and dry foods such as mustard greens or parsley in the same dish or meal. The key to good health was to balance the temperatures and levels of moisture.

Preparation time: about 1 hour

10 young sage leaves
10 young spinach leaves
1/3 cup slivered almonds
1/3 cup seedless raisins
1/3 cup figs, cut in fine strips
1 (2-ounce) jar capers,
    drained
1 cup dried currants
1/2 cup whole black olives
1/4 cup sugar

1. Wash and shake dry the sage and spinach leaves. In a glass salad bowl, mix them together with the almonds, raisins, figs, capers, currants, black olives and sugar.

1 tablespoon olive oil
1 tablespoon red wine
    vinegar
1/2 teaspoon sugar

2. In a small bowl, blend the oil and vinegar. Pour it over the ingredients, and mix well. Sprinkle the 1/2 teaspoon of sugar evenly over the top.

1 orange, peeled and thinly
    sliced
1 lemon, peeled and thinly
    sliced

3. Lay the orange and lemon slices over the mixture in the bowl.

1 (2- to 3-pound) red
    cabbage
1 (6-ounce) jar sliced dill
    pickles
1 head Boston lettuce
1/2 cup whole black olives
1 orange, peeled and thinly
    sliced
1 lemon, peeled and thinly
    sliced

4. Separate the red cabbage leaves, and lay them over the orange and lemon slices. Shred the tender inner leaves of the lettuce. Cover the cabbage with the pickles, olives and shredded lettuce. Arrange the remaining orange and lemon slices on top of the salad.

Serves 6 to 8

TO MAKE SNOW

Take a quart of thicke creame, and five or sixe whites of Egs, a sawcerfull of Rosewater, beate all together, and ever as it riseth take it out with a spoone: then take a loafe of bread, cut away the crust, and set it upright in a platter. Then set a faire great Rosemarie bush in the middest of your bread: then lay your snow with a spoon upon your rosemary, and upon your bread, & gilt it. (The Good Huswifes Handmaide for the Kitchin, 1594)

The "dish of snow" is a perfect example of the Elizabethans' love of decorative foods. The cook laboriously beat the mixture of cream and egg whites with a spoon, a bunch of feathers or a bundle of twigs until it stiffened. Next the branch of rosemary was affixed to a solid base such as a round loaf of bread or an apple, which was placed in the center of a platter. The cream mixture was then used to create a miniature winter landscape of a snow-covered pine atop a hill. While this treat was likely eaten alone in the manner of strawberry shortcake, the "snow" makes a particularly nice topping for A Pruen Tart (see p. 33).

Preparation time: about 20 minutes

1. Beat together the cream, egg whites, sugar and rose water until the mixture is stiff but not dry.

2 cups heavy cream
3 egg whites
¼ cup sugar
3 tablespoons rose water

2. Place the loaf on a serving platter. Set the rosemary branch firmly in the center. Carefully spoon the whipped mixture onto and around the bread, and place small dollops on the twigs of the rosemary branch.

1 small, round loaf of bread, crust removed
1 branch rosemary

Serves 6 to 8

TO BAKE A TENCH WITH A PUDDING IN HER BELLY

Let your Fish blood in the tayle, then scalde it, and scowre it: wash it cleane and drie it with a cloth. Then take grated Bread, sweet Creame, the yolkes of two or three new laid Egges, a few parboyled Currins, and a fewe sweet Hearbes, chopt fine. Season it with Nutmeg, and Pepper, and make it into a stiffe Pudding, & put it into your Tenches belly. Season your Fish on the outside, with a little Pepper, Salt, and Nutmeg, and so put him in a deepe Coffin, with a piece of sweet butter, and so close our Pye, and bake it. Then take it out of the Oven, and open it, and cast in a piece of preserved Orenge minst. Then take Vinegar, Nutmeg, Butter, Sugar, and the yolke of a new layd Egge, and boyle it on a Chafingdish of coales, always stirring it to keepe it from curding: then pour it into your Pye, shogge it well together, and serve it in. (John Murrell, A New Booke of Cookerie, 1615)

The tench is an English freshwater fish, but this preparation, like most period recipes, is equally good for other sorts of fish. "Puddings in the belly," which we would call stuffings, were popular in Pilgrim times. A pudding could be several things: a sausage, a stuffing or farcing mixture or a grain-based boiled preparation. In each case, chopped mixtures of ingredients were put into a container, such as a skin, a fish or a mold, and then cooked.

In the seventeenth century baked goods were encased in crusts ("coffins"). Some crusts were to be eaten; others were simply disposable containers in which foods were cooked and served.

Preparation time: about 50 minutes

2 cups dry bread crumbs, preferably homemade
2 egg yolks, well beaten
1/4 cup dried currants
1/2 teaspoon thyme
1/2 teaspoon marjoram
1/4 teaspoon freshly grated nutmeg
1/4 teaspoon freshly ground black pepper
2 to 6 tablespoons light cream

1. Preheat the oven to 350 degrees.
2. To make the "pudding," combine in a bowl the bread crumbs, egg yolks, currants, thyme, marjoram, nutmeg, pepper and 2 tablespoons cream. Mix well. Continue to add cream by the tablespoonful, mixing well after each addition, until the stuffing is moistened thoroughly.

1 whole cod or haddock (3 to 4 pounds), cleaned

3. Stuff the fish with the "pudding," and set it aside.

1 recipe Flaky Pie Pastry (see p. 183)

4. Roll the pastry into a large square, and cut it into two rectangular pieces, one half the size of the other. Place the fish carefully onto the center of the larger piece, and fold the sides up

around the fish. Cover with the smaller piece, snugly encasing the fish. Trim off the excess dough, and seal in the fish by crimping the edges. Mold the pastry into a fish shape, and decorate it with fins and scales made out of leftover dough. The vent holes may be cut as gills.

5. Transfer the fish pie to a baking sheet. Bake the pie for 30 minutes, or until it bubbles.

6. Near the end of the baking period, prepare the sauce. In a small saucepan, melt the butter over low heat. Stir in the orange peel, vinegar, egg yolk, nutmeg and sugar. Stirring constantly to prevent curdling, continue cooking the sauce over low heat until it has thickened and is warmed through. Pour the sauce into the pie through the vents, and shake the pie gently to distribute the sauce throughout. Serve hot.

Serves 6 to 8

1 tablespoon unsalted butter
1 tablespoon finely chopped
   candied orange peel
¼ cup malt vinegar
1 egg yolk, well beaten
½ teaspoon freshly grated
   nutmeg
2 teaspoons sugar

A PRUEN TART

Take of the fairest damaske pruens you can get, and put them in a cleane pipkin with faire water, suger, unbruised cinamon, and a branch or two of Rosemarie; and if you have bread to bake, stew them in the oven with your bread; if otherwise, stew them on the fire: when they are stewed, then bruise them all to mash in their sirrop, and straine them into a cleane dish; then boyle it over againe with suger, sinamon, and rosewater till it bee as thicke as Marmalad; then set it to coole, then make a reasonable tuffe paste with fine flower, water, and a little butter, and rowle it out very thin; then having patterns of paper cut in divers proportions, as Beasts, Birds, Armes, Knots, Flowers, and such like; lay the patterns on the paste, and so cut them accordingly; then with your fingers pinch up the edges of the paste, and set the worke in good proportion: then prick it well all over for rising, and set it on a cleane sheete of large paper, and so set it into the Oven, and bake it hard: then draw it, and set it to coole: and thus you may doe by a whole Oven full at once, as your occasion of expence is: then against the time of service comes, take off the confection of pruens before rehearsed, and with your knife, or a spoone fill the coffin according to the thickness of the verge: then strow it all over with caraway comfets, and pricke long comfets upright in it, and so taking the paper from the bottome, serve it on a plate in a dish or charger, according to the bigness of the tarte (Gervase Markham, *Countrey Contentments*, 1623)

Dried fruit played an important part in the cuisine of seventeenth-century Europeans. At a time when sugar was rare and costly, the natural sweetening provided by currants, raisins, dates and prunes was much appreciated. In addition, dried fruit provided a welcome variation in the winter, when bread, salted meat and fish, and beer made for a tedious diet. The English colonists brought their taste for dried fruit to the New World and not only imported currants and prunes by the barrel, but also traded with the Indians for dried blueberries.

Dried fruits might be eaten with nuts at the end of a meal, but they were most often used in cooking, as in meat pies or in winter tarts. The decorative crust cut with the aid of paper patterns was a typical whimsy of the period, but the pastry figures also helped identify the contents of the pie.

Preparation time: about 1 hour

1 recipe Flaky Pie Pastry
(see. p. 183)

1. Preheat the oven to 450 degrees.

2. Roll out half the pastry, and from it cut out four circles 6 inches in diameter. Repeat with the remaining pastry dough. Transfer the pastry to eight small tart pans, and crimp the edges. Place the pastry shells on a baking sheet, and prick the dough all over with the tines of a fork. Bake the shells for 12 to 15 minutes, or until they are lightly browned. Cool them on a rack.

2 pounds pitted prunes
1 cup water
¼ cup sugar
1 teaspoon cinnamon
1 teaspoon rosemary
¼ cup rose water

3. In a medium saucepan, combine the prunes, water, sugar, cinnamon and rosemary, and bring the mixture to a boil. Reduce the heat, and simmer for 10 minutes, or until the prunes are very soft. Remove the pan from the heat, and mash the mixture. Stir in the rose water, return the pan to low heat, and simmer for 10 minutes longer. The mixture should have the consistency of jam.

¼ cup candied caraway
seeds (available at Near
Eastern food shops)

4. Spoon the prune mixture into the prepared shells, and sprinkle with the caraway seeds. Let the tarts cool before serving.

Makes 8 tarts

IV

The Food of the Wampanoag

BY THE STAFF OF PLIMOTH PLANTATION

Wampanoag Foodways

The Wampanoag ("Eastern People") still live in southeastern Massachusetts and eastern Rhode Island, where their ancestors met the Pilgrims over 350 years ago. The dishes that the Wampanoag enjoyed in the 1620s were quite unlike any that modern Americans know. Although they used some foods we enjoy today, such as squash, beans, pumpkins, turkeys and lobsters, the absence of salt, sugar, spices, yeast breads, alcohol and dairy products made the Indian diet very different from ours. Re-creating such an extinct cuisine is a difficult research problem. The introduction of foods and tastes into New England from the rest of the world thoroughly obscured the earlier traditions, and the historic record doesn't always tell researchers what they need to know. Nevertheless, we do have a general overview of the diet of the Wampanoag in the time of the Pilgrims.

The food of the Wampanoag reflected a thorough dependence on local resources. Virtually everything they ate came from the immediate area, and their husbanding of these resources was central to their interaction with their environment. As has often been observed, the Wampanoag developed a very efficient and effective system for drawing what they needed from the land without destructive exploitation of the resources. As Samuel de Champlain observed in 1616, before the Pilgrims arrived, the Wampanoag were quite content with their situation and did not envy the Europeans with whom they had come in contact. "They . . . are happy among themselves, not having experienced anything better, and not imagining that anything more excellent is to be found," he wrote in his *Voyages*. However, historical (and romantic) hindsight should not obscure the fact that this ecological position was a natural part of their culture rather than any conscious decision to respect "Mother Earth."

The Wampanoag practiced agriculture as well as hunting, fishing and gathering wild foods. Corn was the primary field crop around which other crops, such as beans of different sorts and the local squash and pumpkins, were grown. The Wampanoag raised both soft flour corn and a hard flint "feed"-type corn, both of which came in many colors, but not popcorn. Like corn, local kidney-type beans came in a variety of colors. The corn and the beans were easily dried and stored, and they provided a nourishing diet. The squashes and pumpkins were seasonally important as a prolific food source, but they were harder to preserve through drying and were less important in the Wampanoag diet than the corn and beans. It is difficult to be sure what sorts of squashes were available, but they probably included the summer, crookneck, bush scallop, acorn and hubbard varieties, as well as a small round one known as the apple squash and, of course, the pumpkin. The Wampanoag also raised small round watermelons and jerusalem artichokes. The tubers of the jerusalem artichoke (now sold in markets as "sun chokes") may have been gathered from the wild as well as cultivated. The Wampanoag also cultivated the regular sunflower, and used the seeds for food.

Plant foods the Wampanoag gathered rather than raised included the spring shoots of such plants as milkweed, poke, cattail and skunk cabbage; flowers such as milkweed, pumpkin, and the cattail's pollen tip; roots and tubers such as groundnuts, arrowhead tubers, cattail, bulrush root knobs, sweet flag and pond lily roots; berries including the strawberry, blueberry, huckleberry, raspberry, blackberry, wild black cherry, cranberry and boxberry (wintergreen or checkerberry); fruits such as beach plums, wild plums and wild grapes; nuts of the hazel, hickory, black walnut, beech and butternut trees, and white oak acorns. Plants used as flavorings included wild ginger, sarsaparilla root, sassafras root, and possibly other leaves and wild onions.

The various edible berries and fruits in the area were gathered and used in season, both raw and cooked, and preserved by drying, either as individual berries (like raisins) or in cakes of pounded and dried pulp to be used in cooking. John Josselyn, a seventeenth-century English visitor to New England, mentions the trade between the English and the Indians for dried blueberries, which the Indians sold by the bushel. Cranberries, which were not cultivated anywhere until after 1800, were among the fruits that were dried, although their sourness made them relatively unpopular at a time when they could not be used with sugar by either the Europeans or the Indians. (There is no evidence that the Wampanoag used maple sugar, although Indians of northern New England did.) Still, cranberries were used in breads and mixed with dried meat. When sugar became commonly available around 1650, cranberries became the basis for a popular sauce, as they are today. Other fruits, such as the beach plum or wild cherry, were also used either fresh or in a preserved form.

Cooked food was preferred to raw food. Neither the Wampanoag nor the English colonists of the period shared the modern taste for raw salads and lightly cooked foods (although the Indians did eat things raw at times, from berries and chestnuts to bulrush roots and eggs). The fundamental cooking methods were boiling, roasting and grilling. There is no evidence that the Wampanoag fried foods in fat, steamed them, or baked them in containers (except for leaves, in which they wrapped foods before burying them in residual coals) or ovens. Boiling was the least labor-intensive method of cooking, as roasting took more care, but the Wampanoag, like other people, often preferred the result of the less efficient method.

Except for such shellfish as the women could gather on their own at the seashore, meat and fish were the men's contribution to the Indian diet. The most important meat source was deer, which were hunted in large numbers during the winter. Venison was eaten fresh or carefully dried for later use, while the bones, sinew and hides were saved to make tools and clothing. Bears were prized for their flavorful fat, and many other woodland animals were shot by skillful Indian bowmen or trapped with deadfalls. Fowl, including turkeys, geese and ducks, also played an important role in

Wampanoag cuisine. From the late fall until planting time, Wampanoag men endured arduous chases and cold days without food or rest to provide their families with food and clothing.

Corn played a major role in Wampanoag cookery. We are most familiar with the dry-ground meal processed directly from the kernels, but the Indians used other methods of preparation as well. Green or unripe field corn was used fresh in a milky or unripe condition; it was boiled on the ear or scraped from the ear as we scrape the kernels from sweet corn to make creamed corn (although green corn is different from true sweet corn, which is thought to have been introduced into New England from the Iroquois in the eighteenth century). Green corn was also boiled in a succotash-like mixture (including the broken-up cobs), baked in leaves, and made into cakes.

The uses for ripe corn depended on its type. Flint corns were boiled with lye or wood ashes to swell the kernel and loosen the hulls. The kernels were then rinsed, and the hulls were washed and rubbed off. The dried corn was pounded in a mortar and sifted into finer meal for boiled or baked bread, leaving the coarse meal for boiled samp (mush), or it was cooked whole as hulled corn (today sold canned as "whole hominy"). The flour corns were parched for later use. This process exposed the corn kernels to heat so that they puffed slightly, like half-popped popcorn, and could be easily ground into a fine, easily preserved flour.

The most common recipes of the Indians of southeastern New England were corn-based soups to which meat or fish were added. "Msickquatash" (hence "succotash," or boiled corn soup) was a basic staple dish, like a stew with many variations. In its simplest form, it was just corn and beans. It could contain boiled green corn, boiled cornmeal, or boiled hulled corn and beans. The beans were cooked fresh or reconstituted from dried supplies. Venison, fish, rabbit, some sort of fat, roots and wild onions might be added. Meats and fish were also roasted or grilled separately and served with it.

In Wampanoag meals, women cooked the food and left it for the men, who always ate first. As soon as the men were through, the women and children entered the house and helped themselves to what was left, which was generally ample. The Wampanoag apparently ate two meals a day: breakfast before noon, after early-morning work, and dinner in the evening, after the day's work was over. Between these two roughly defined mealtimes, people ate small snacks at random rather than clearly defined formal meals. Service was, of course, simple, much like a picnic or camp meal, as William Wood described in *New England's Prospect* (1634):

Some of their scullery [female cooks] having dressed these homely cates [food, as in catering], presents it to his guests, dishing it up in a rude manner, placing it on the verdant carpet of the earth which nature spreads them, without either trenchers, napkins, or knives, upon which their hunger-sauced stomachs, impatient of delays, falls aboard without scrupling at unwashed hands, without bread, salt, or beer, lolling on the Turkish fashion, not ceasing till their full bellies leave nothing but empty platters.

Another characteristic of Wampanoag meals was the free generosity with which guests and casual drop-ins were fed along with the family.

In re-creating everyday Indian meals, do not be misled by the modern custom of providing a large number of separate dishes, but rather prepare a main dish such as hulled corn or samp soup, with a number of pieces of meat or fish, or other roasted items (such as fresh corn on the cob or squash) and perhaps bread, as extra. Guests should help themselves (by hand, skewer or ladle) to food from the center pot or serving bowl and eat one helping at a time, rather than arranging separate portions together on a plate. Pieces of roasted meat or fish should be either eaten with the fingers or speared from the pot with bone or wooden skewers, while broth should be drunk from the spoon or bowl after the solid items are gone.

Seventeenth-Century Wampanoag Recipes

Their food is generally boiled maize, or Indian corn, mixed with kidney-beans, or sometimes without. Also they frequently boil in this pottage fish or flesh of all sorts, either new taken or dried, as shads, eels, alewives or a sort of herring, or any other sort of fish. . . . These they cut in pieces, bones and all, and boil them in the aforesaid pottage. Also they boil in this furmety all sorts of flesh they take in hunting; as venison, beaver, bear's flesh, moose, otters, rackoons, or any kind they take in hunting; cutting this flesh into small pieces, and boiling it as aforesaid. Also they mix with the said pottage several sorts of roots, and pompions, and squashes and also several sorts of nuts or masts, as oak-acorns, chestnuts, walnuts; these husked and dried, and powdered, they thicken their pottage therewith. (Daniel Gookin, *Historical Collections of the Indians of New England*, 1792)

Period Indian recipes are more general than modern ones and lack definite measurements. Like an ethnic cook preparing a spaghetti sauce or a boiled dinner, one simply knew how to do it; the general parameters were all that mattered. One used what one had. It made little difference whether one or two fish were used, or whether there was 2 or 10 pounds of meat to cook. The lack of seasonings such as salt, sugar and spices meant that proportions of ingredients were far less important to acceptable flavor than in modern recipes. For the benefit of modern cooks, however, general proportions for the recipes are provided here.

Another characteristic of period Indian cooking is that many of the dishes will taste bland to the modern palate. They are nevertheless quite good and certainly healthy. If you wish to modify these recipes to suit the contemporary taste for salt or sugar, you may add seasonings at the end of the cooking. Most people will find that the fish dishes prepared with clam broth are salty enough as they are. A piece of butter added in the meat soup will parallel the Indian practice of adding deer or bear fat to such recipes, and will provide extra savor as well.

These recipes are designed for the resources of the contemporary cook, and therefore contain appropriate substitutes for the wild food and game available to the seventeenth-century Wampanoag. For the cook who wishes to attempt a more authentic version, however, the original ingredient is noted in each case. Familiar recipes such as johnnycake or standard succotash are not included, as these are easily available, nor have we provided any recipe for roasted or grilled meats and fish, foods too basic to require any recipe at all. Any of these dishes may be accompanied with grilled game or fish, cooked without salt, pepper or sauce.

HOMINY OR HULLED CORN

Whole hominy or hulled corn, as New Englanders called it, may be bought today in cans. For the more solid and flavorful homemade kind, here are some suggestions.

Preparation time: about 8 hours

1. Since you will be working with lye, you *must* use a clay or iron pot and only wooden implements. In the clay or iron pot, bring the water to a boil. Add a double handful of fine hardwood ashes, and boil until the liquid will float an egg.

3 quarts water

2. In a saucepan, boil the flint corn (or any feed corn) in 3 quarts water for an hour or so.

1 quart flint corn
3 quarts water

3. Drain the corn, and add it to the lye solution. Boil until the kernels swell and the hulls loosen.

4. Drain off the lye, and dispose of it down the drain. Rinse the corn in clear water several times so it is clean and safe to work with; rub off and discard the hulls with the wash water. Add fresh water, and bring to a boil. Boil the hulled corn for at least 4 hours; then use it for cooking or store it in fresh water to cover.

Makes about a gallon, depending on how long you boil the corn

CORN SOUP AND MEAT (OR FOWL)

This recipe is based on the many descriptions of whole corn soups or stews found in historic accounts. The meat can be added either to the cold water at the beginning, to provide a stronger broth, or to the simmering broth towards the end of cooking, for more flavorful meat.

Preparation time: about 2 hours

2 pounds lamb or venison
shanks or a 2½-pound
chicken, cut in pieces
2 cups (about 6 ounces) ½-
inch cubed butternut or
other winter squash
½ cup small white pearl
onions
1 quart water (or more if
necessary)

1. Cut the meat from the bones. Cut the meat into 1-inch chunks. Put the meat, bones, squash and onions into the cold water, and bring to a boil. Reduce the heat to a simmer, and cook for ½ hour.

¾ cup walnuts (instead of
native black walnuts or
other wild nuts)
1 (16-ounce) can whole
hominy or 2½ to 3 cups
homemade hominy (see
page 41)
1 (16-ounce) can red kidney
beans
¼ cup chopped cranberries

2. Grind the walnuts to a powder in a blender or food processor. Add the ground walnuts, hominy, beans and cranberries to the soup. Simmer 1 hour.

Serves 4 to 6

CLAM BROTH

Clam broth (or "juice") may be bought in 8-ounce bottles, but you may wish to make your own.

Preparation time: about 15 minutes

1 pound steamer or soft-
shell clams
4 cups water

1. Place the clams in a large saucepan, and cover them with the water. Bring the water to a boil, lower the heat and cook the clams, covered, for 10 minutes (overcooking helps the broth but toughens the clams.) Mince the clams, and save them for another use.
2. Strain the clam broth through a double thickness of cheese cloth to remove the grit.

Makes 4 cups

CORN SOUP AND FISH

This is essentially the same recipe as the meat corn soup, but with fish.

Preparation time: about 1 1/2 hours

1. Cut the jerusalem artichokes into 1-inch sections. In a pot, combine the jerusalem artichokes, hominy, beans and clam broth. Bring to a boil; then reduce the heat to a simmer and cook for about an hour, until the soup is thickened. Add water—not more broth—if the soup is too thick.

1 pound jerusalem artichokes, scrubbed
1 (16-ounce) can whole hominy or 2 1/2 to 3 cups homemade hominy (see page 41)
1 (16-ounce) can small red kidney beans
2 cups clam broth (see page 42)

2. Cut the fish into 1-inch chunks. Add the fish to the soup, return the soup to a simmer, and cook for 10 minutes. Serve hot.

1 pound cod or pollock fillets (Or: 1 eel, cut in 2-inch sections; 2 pounds soft-shell clams, shucked and cleaned or 3 (6-ounce) cans chopped clams; 1 lobster in the shell, cut in pieces).

Serves 4 to 6

SAMP AND FISH

They take the pounded Indian corn, without removing the bran, and put two or three handfuls of it in an earthen pot full of water. This they boil, stirring it from time to time, that it may not burn nor adhere to the pot. Then they put in a pot a small quantity of fish, fresh or dry, according to season, to give a flavor. . . . (Samuel de Champlain, Voyages of Samuel de Champlain, 1604–1618)

This dish is similar to the corn soup, but is made with cornmeal rather than whole hominy. It is important to use the bones and skin of the fish for flavor.

Preparation time: about 45 minutes

1½ cups clam broth (see page 42)
1 small whole fish (about 1 pound), gutted and cut in 3-inch pieces

1. Bring the broth to a boil. Add the fish pieces—skin, head, and all—and simmer for 5 minutes. Strain and reserve the broth. When the fish has cooled, remove the flesh from the bones and skin. Return the flesh to the broth, and reserve.

1½ cups water
1½ cups clam broth (see page 42)
1 cup coarse cornmeal (masa harina, available at Hispanic specialty stores)
1 (16-ounce) can small red kidney beans
¼ cup ground walnuts

2. Combine the broth and water. Pour the cornmeal into the mixture, and simmer, stirring frequently, until the meal is soft, about 15 minutes. Add the reserved fish, the beans and the ground walnuts to the meal, and bring the mixture to a simmer before serving.

Serves 4 to 6

SAMP AND FRUIT

From this meal they make bread, using also beans which they first boil, as they do the Indian corn for soup, so that they may be more easily crushed. Then they mix all together, sometimes adding blueberries . . . (Samuel de Champlain, *Voyages of Samuel de Champlain*, 1604–1618)

Samp and Fruit is a sweet porridge made from boiled cornmeal and native fruit such as strawberries, blueberries or plums. Frozen fruits are also suitable.

Preparation time: about 30 minutes

In a 1- to 2-quart saucepan, bring the water to a boil. Slowly add the cornmeal, and cook for 15 minutes, stirring frequently. Add the fresh or thawed fruit, and cook slowly for 10 minutes, still stirring frequently, until the fruit is reduced to a pulp and permeates the porridge. The dish may be served hot, as porridge, or thickened, cooled, and sliced.

3 cups water
1 cup coarse cornmeal
   (masa harina, *available*
   at Hispanic specialty
   stores)
1 cup fresh blueberries, or 1
   cup frozen berries,
   thawed

Serves 6

BOILED BREAD

They sometimes beat their maize into meal, and sift it through a basket, made for that purpose. With this meal they make bread, baking it in the ashes, covering the dough with leaves. Sometimes they make of their meal a small sort of cakes, and boil them. (Daniel Gookin, *Historical Collections of the Indians of New England*, 1792)

Roger Williams noted that Wampanoag bread was sometimes boiled in clam broth to add flavor. The water left after the cakes were cooked, cloudy with the extra starch from the dough, was drunk as a beverage.

Preparation time: about 30 minutes

1. Mix the two cornmeals together. Add the beans, walnuts and sunflower seeds, and mix all together. Pour the boiling water over the ingredients, and stir until the mixture can be molded into a soft cake about 6 inches in diameter and 2 inches thick.
2. Once the cake is shaped, clean your hands and wet them in cold water; then smooth the surface of the bread.

1 cup coarse cornmeal
   (masa harina, *available*
   at Hispanic specialty
   stores)
1 cup fine cornmeal
1/2 cup canned red kidney
   beans, mashed
1/4 cup ground walnuts
1/4 cup shelled sunflower
   seeds
1 cup boiling water

8 cups water

3. In a 3- to 4-quart saucepan, bring the water to a boil. Drop the bread gently into the boiling water. When the bread floats (after about 10 minutes), boil it for another 10 minutes, until it is done. Remove it from the water with a slotted spoon or spoons, and serve.

Serves 4

V

Breads and Muffins

CORNBREAD

Corn was among the first new foods the Pilgrims encountered in Massachusetts, and before long it became one of their most important crops. Although it could have been consumed half-grown, as "green" corn, similar to sweet corn today, the Pilgrims found it more useful when ground into flour and meal, staples to sustain them through long winters. As the colonial period progressed, corn mills powered by water or horses sprang up throughout New England. Some of them—among them the Old Mill on Nantucket, the mill beside Sandwich Town Hall, and Plymouth's own Jenney Grist Mill—have been restored, and visitors today can buy samples of their wares to use in their own baking back home.

Cornbread is often considered a Southern specialty (and with good reason), but New Englanders, too, have made it for many years. Thanks to the revival of regional American cooking, cornbread is enjoying a resurgence in popularity.

Although cornbread is not difficult to make, it *can* fall flat, as the Pilgrim housewives discovered when they tried adapting the wheat-bread recipes they had brought from England to gluten-free corn flour. Three secrets: Start with a sizzling-hot pan; blend the ingredients with as few strokes as possible; and, if possible, use buttermilk or sour milk.

This basic batter, adapted from the recipe used at Boston's Durgin-Park restaurant, can be used not only for breads but, with reduced baking times, for muffins and sticks as well.

Preparation time: about 45 minutes

1. Preheat the oven to 425 degrees. Generously butter an 11- by 7-inch baking pan, and place it in the oven to get hot.

2 eggs, beaten
²/₃ cup sugar

2. Meanwhile, in a large bowl, beat together the eggs and sugar.

2 cups yellow cornmeal
1 cup flour
1 tablespoon baking powder
³/₄ teaspoon salt
3 tablespoons unsalted butter, melted
1¹/₂ cups buttermilk

3. Sift together the cornmeal, flour, baking powder and salt into a bowl. Stir the dry ingredients into the egg mixture. Add the butter and buttermilk, and combine with a few rapid strokes. Do not overbeat; the batter should be somewhat lumpy.

4. Remove the hot pan from the oven, and pour in the batter. Bake for about 25 minutes, or until a knife inserted in the center comes out clean. Cool on a rack for 15 minutes before cutting the cornbread into squares.

Serves 10 to 12

SPIDER CORNBREAD

The name *spider* in this recipe comes, happily, not from an ingredient but from the type of pan in which the bread used to be baked in the old days. A heavy, covered cast-iron skillet with three short legs, the "spider" was ideal for setting over glowing coals in an open fireplace. This cornbread recipe, with its unusual custardy texture, was given to me by the Brewster family of Plymouth, who traditionally serve it with steamed lobster.

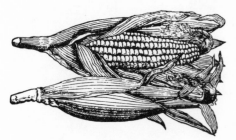

Preparation time: about 1¹/4 hours

1. Preheat the oven to 400 degrees.
2. Place the butter in a 9-inch cast iron "spider" or skillet, and set the pan in the oven. When the butter has melted, swirl it around to coat the bottom and sides of the pan. Remove it from the heat, and set it aside.

3 tablespoons unsalted butter

3. While the butter is melting, combine the cornmeal, flour, sugar, baking powder and salt in a strainer, and sift them into a mixing bowl.

1¹/2 cups cornmeal
¹/2 cup flour
¹/4 cup sugar
2 teaspoons baking powder
1 teaspoon salt

4. In a small mixing bowl, beat the eggs until frothy. Add the sour and "sweet" milks, and blend well. Beat in the melted butter from the skillet.

2 eggs
1 cup sour milk (or 1 cup milk mixed with 1 tablespoon white vinegar)
1 cup milk

5. Pour the milk mixture into the cornmeal, and mix until well blended. (The batter will be very runny.) Pour the batter into the hot buttered skillet.
6. Bake the cornbread for 5 minutes.
7. Without stirring, pour the last 1 cup of milk over the surface of the cornbread as it is baking. Bake the cake 45 minutes longer.

1 cup milk

8. Remove the bread from the oven. Run a knife around the edge to loosen it. Serve it warm, cut in wedges.

Serves 6

CORNMEAL PANCAKES

In the early years, corn was the principal grain consumed in New England, and it was eaten mostly as a bread, by some as often as three times a day. One form, "johnnycake," was a kind of dense cornmeal pancake, best when made from a hard variety of corn called flint. Tastes change, though, and what our forebears enjoyed is not necessarily what we in New England would relish today. This recipe for Cornmeal Pancakes is an attempt to marry the colonial concept with modern culinary tastes.

Preparation time: about 20 minutes

1 cup flour
1 cup cornmeal
1 tablespoon baking powder
1/2 teaspoon salt

2 eggs
1 1/2 cups milk
1/4 cup heavy cream
2 tablespoons unsalted
    butter, melted

Butter
Maple syrup
Honey

1. Warm the griddle over high heat.
2. Combine the flour, cornmeal, baking powder and salt in a strainer, and sift them into a large mixing bowl.

3. In a small mixing bowl, beat the eggs until they are frothy. Add the milk, cream and melted butter, and beat until the ingredients are well blended.
4. Pour the egg mixture onto the dry ingredients, and beat until the batter is well mixed.

5. Lightly grease the griddle with a vegetable oil spray or butter. Pour about 1/4 cup batter on the griddle for each pancake, and bake about 1 minute each side. The cakes should be bubbly on top and dry around the edges when turned. Serve them hot, with a lump of butter on each pancake and a generous pouring of maple syrup or honey over each serving.

Makes about 18 pancakes

BROWN BREAD

Best known as the accompaniment to baked beans (see page 132), brown bread—with its three grains and generous quantity of molasses—was traditionally steamed for hours in a coffee or baking powder can and then cut with a tautly held string. Today a 9-by-5-inch loaf pan will do admirably, and using a knife is permissible. This recipe even gives you a choice of steaming the bread for three hours or baking it in one-third the time. Steaming remains preferable—the bread rises higher and develops a moist, chewy texture—but if you're pressed for time, feel free to bake. One nontraditional serving suggestion: Leftover brown bread makes a delicious vehicle for cream cheese at breakfast time.

Preparation time: about 3¹/₂ hours

1. Place a rack in a large enameled or stainless steel pot (such as a Dutch oven or wok). Pour in enough water to cover the rack by about 1 inch. Over high heat, bring the water to a boil. Butter a 9-by-5-inch loaf pan or two 1-pound coffee cans, as well as lengths of aluminum foil that will cover and seal the pan or cans.

2. Meanwhile, sift the flour, cornmeal, graham (or whole-wheat) flour and salt together into a large bowl.

1 cup rye flour
1 cup yellow cornmeal
1 cup graham (or whole-wheat) flour
1 teaspoon salt

3. In a small bowl, mix the baking soda into the molasses until the mixture foams. Add the buttermilk, and mix well.

1 teaspoon baking soda
³/₄ cup unsulphured molasses
2 cups buttermilk

4. Stir the buttermilk mixture into the dry ingredients; then add the raisins and mix until they are well distributed.

1 cup seedless raisins

5. Pour the batter into the pan or cans. Cover tightly with the buttered foil, securing with string if necessary. (The rising bread can push off the cover.) Place the pan or cans on the steamer rack, and cover the pot tightly. Steam for 3 hours, replenishing the water as necessary.

Serves 8 to 10

BAKED BROWN BREAD

Preparation time: about 1¹/₂ hours

1. Preheat the oven to 350 degrees. Butter a 9-by-5-inch loaf pan and a length of foil to cover the pan.

2. Mix the ingredients as described in steps 2 through 4 above. Pour the batter into the loaf pan. Cover with the buttered foil.

3. Bake for about 1 hour, until a knife inserted in the center comes out clean.

Serves 8 to 10

CRANBERRY-ORANGE-NUT BREAD

"Quick" breads—that is, breads leavened with baking powder or soda rather than yeast—are always popular, because of their ease of preparation. This one starts filling New England kitchens with tempting aromas each fall almost as soon as the first cranberries arrive in the markets, fresh from the bogs. Thanks to the food processor, it may be the quickest "quick" bread of them all. The bread is best served warm. In fact, it rarely lasts long enough to cool down. Its sweet flavor and nutty richness make butter superfluous.

Preparation time: about 1 1/4 hours

1. Preheat the oven to 350 degrees. Generously butter a 9-by-5-inch loaf pan.
2. In a food processor fitted with a steel blade, or by hand, coarsely chop the cranberries and set them aside. Next chop the walnuts, taking care not to chop them too fine. Reserve them.
3. Replace the steel blade of the processor, if you are using one, with the plastic mixing blade. Place the flour, sugar, baking powder, baking soda and salt in the bowl of the processor, and whirl until they are well mixed. Add the orange juice, rind, shortening and egg, and whirl until the batter is well blended, but do not overwork it. (The batter will be pink at this stage, but the coloration will disappear during the baking.) Or mix the ingredients, in the same order, in an electric mixer or by hand.
4. Pour the batter into the loaf pan and bake 50 to 60 minutes, or until a toothpick inserted in the center comes out clean. Cool 15 minutes on a rack before removing the bread from the pan. Serve warm, cut in thick slices.

Makes 1 (9-by-5-inch) loaf

1 1/2 cups cranberries
1/2 cup walnut halves

2 cups flour
1 cup sugar
*1 1/2 teaspoons baking
    powder*
1/2 teaspoon baking soda
1 teaspoon salt
*3/4 cup strained fresh orange
    juice*
*1 teaspoon grated orange
    rind*
*2 tablespoons vegetable
    shortening*
1 egg

MOLASSES DOUGHNUTS

There once was a lady named Sophie Saunders, who lived in West Chatham, on Cape Cod, alone except for a retinue of cats of all colors, shapes and characters. She dwelt on the crest of a hill in an old Victorian farmhouse that had obviously seen better days, for its roof sagged ominously, the green shutters at the windows hung lopsided, and the paint on the white clapboard was peeling badly. But nothing seemed to faze Sophie, who supplemented whatever other meager income she had by making the best doughnuts under the most elemental of conditions, with pots of melted lard smoking on her wood stove. Her following was legion, and I can't describe the disappointment I would feel if my mother and I arrived at Sophie's only to find she had sold out for the day. She never gave out her recipe, and she never measured, but her hands never failed her. This recipe is not hers, unfortunately. Would that it were. But I dedicate it to Sophie, and I include it to remind people just how good homemade doughnuts can be.

Preparation time: about 3½ hours

1. Sift the flour, nutmeg, cinnamon and baking soda into a large mixing bowl.

6 cups flour
1 teaspoon freshly grated nutmeg
1 teaspoon cinnamon
1 tablespoon baking soda

2. In another large bowl, beat the eggs until they are thick and light, then gradually beat in the sugar, molasses and butter. Add the buttermilk, and mix until the ingredients are well combined. In four parts, add the flour mixture, beating until each addition is well incorporated. Cover the bowl with plastic wrap, and refrigerate the dough for at least 2 hours, or overnight if possible.

3 eggs
1 cup sugar
½ cup unsulphured molasses
3 tablespoons unsalted butter, melted
1 cup buttermilk

3. In a deep fryer or deep, heavy pot, preheat the shortening to 360 degrees.

Vegetable shortening for deep frying

4. Have at hand 2 cookie sheets or jelly roll pans, preferably the nonstick variety.

5. Cut off about ⅓ of the dough, and return the remaining to the refrigerator. On a lightly floured surface, with a floured rolling pin, roll the dough out to a thickness of ⅓ inch. Working quickly so that the dough remains chilled, cut out doughnuts using a 2¾-inch doughnut cutter. As they are cut, immediately transfer them to one of the cookie sheets. When the cookie sheet is full, place it in the refrigerator for 10 minutes for the dough to chill. Repeat, filling the second sheet, until the first batch of dough has been used. Reroll the scraps once, but not twice, as the dough will toughen with too much rolling. Use a 1-inch cutter to form doughnut balls out of the remaining scraps.

6. Deep-fry four or five doughnuts at a time, turning them with a slotted spoon after they have fried for 2 minutes on the first side. Fry them about 1 minute on the second side. When done, they should be puffed and golden brown. Drain the doughnuts on paper towelling.

1 to 2 cups sugar

7. Pour 1 cup of sugar into a brown paper bag. Add four or five still-hot doughnuts, close the bag and shake well to coat them with sugar. (Add more sugar to the bag as needed.) Transfer them to platters or plates to cool as you fry, drain and sugar the rest.

8. Repeat steps 5 through 7 with the remaining pieces of dough.

Makes about 48 doughnuts and 60 doughnut "holes"

ANADAMA BREAD

Nobody seems certain just how the name *anadama* evolved. One tale has it that Anna was a fine baker, whose husband, praising her, referred to her as "Anna, damn her," a rather unusual form of endearment. Another has her an incompetent baker with a husband who, when his patience was exhausted, felt called upon to make the family bread himself. According to legend, when he finally sat down to eat it he growled, "Anna, damn her!"

Preparation time: 3¼ hours

1. Pour the warm water into a small, shallow bowl. Stir in the sugar. Sprinkle the yeast over the surface. Let the mixture proof for 10 minutes. If the yeast is not bubbling at the end of that time, discard the mixture and repeat the process with fresh yeast.

1/2 cup warm water (about 110 degrees)
1 tablespoon sugar
2 packages dry yeast

2. Pour the water into a small saucepan. Add the butter and molasses. Over moderate heat, stir the mixture until the butter melts. Remove the saucepan from the heat, and allow it to cool to lukewarm.

1 cup water
4 tablespoons unsalted butter
1/2 cup unsulphured molasses

3. Combine the proofed yeast and the butter-and-molasses mixture in a large bowl. Beat in the cornmeal, salt and 4 cups of flour, 1 cup at a time. With a large wooden spoon, continue to beat the mixture vigorously until it is well blended. Turn the dough out on a floured surface, and knead in the remaining 1 cup flour. Continue to knead the dough for 10 minutes, or until it is smooth and elastic.

1/2 cup cornmeal, preferably stone-ground
2 teaspoons salt
5 cups flour

4. Generously butter another large bowl. Place the ball of dough into the bowl, and turn it over several times until it is completely covered with a thin coating of butter. Cover the bowl with a kitchen towel, and set it aside in a draft-free corner of the kitchen (or an unheated oven), until it doubles in bulk, about 1 1/2 hours.

5. Generously butter two 9-by-5-inch loaf pans. Punch the dough down, and knead it for a couple of minutes. Divide it in half, and shape each half into a loaf. Place the loaves in the pans.

6. In a small bowl, combine the egg yolk and the cream, and whisk them until they are well blended. With a pastry brush, gently paint the wash on the surface of the loaves. Cover the bread with the kitchen towel, and put the loaves in a draft-free spot until the dough has risen to the top of the pans, about 30 minutes.

1 egg yolk, beaten
3 tablespoons light cream

7. Preheat the oven to 375 degrees.

8. Remove the towel from the pans, and bake the bread for 40 minutes, or until it sounds hollow when tapped. Turn the loaves out onto a rack to cool.

Makes 2 loaves

PORTUGUESE SWEET BREAD

While all of America is a vast melting pot of peoples and cultures, many of the traditions and food styles from our countries of origin endure. This is particularly true among the people of Portuguese extraction living in southeastern Massachusetts. (See, for example, our Portuguese-influenced Steamed Mussels with Linguica, p. 88, and Portuguese Kale Soup, p. 74.) Portuguese Sweet Bread is another New England favorite, and devotees will frequently make special trips to the Portuguese bakeries between New Bedford and Provincetown just to buy one of the round, sweet-smelling loaves as it is taken from the oven. Portuguese Sweet Bread resembles French brioche, with the same delicate taste and fine crumb. It is wonderful consumed right out of the oven or else toasted, thickly spread with unsalted butter and a smothering of honey.

Preparation time: about 3 1/2 hours

1 teaspoon sugar
1/2 cup lukewarm water
2 tablespoons dry yeast

1/2 cup milk
1/2 cup unsalted butter, at
room temperature
3/4 cup sugar
2 teaspoons salt
4 eggs, beaten

6 to 8 cups flour

1. In a large mixing bowl, dissolve the sugar in the water. Sprinkle the yeast over the water, and allow it to proof. If the yeast is not bubbling after 10 minutes, discard the mixture and repeat the process with fresh yeast.

2. In a small saucepan, put the milk, butter, sugar and salt. Over low heat, heat the mixture to lukewarm. Stir until the butter and sugar dissolve. If the mixture gets too hot, cool it to lukewarm. Then beat in the eggs.

3. Add the tepid milk mixture to the yeast, and stir to combine.

4. One cup at a time, beat 6 cups of flour into the liquid ingredients. The dough should be slightly sticky. If it seems too sticky, add up to 1 cup more flour. Turn the dough out onto a floured surface, and knead in 1/2 to 1 cup more flour. (Moisture in the flour and atmosphere makes a great difference in the amount of flour needed for Portuguese Sweet Bread.) Continue to knead the dough for 10 minutes, or until it is smooth and elastic. It will be very soft, pliable dough.

5. Generously butter a large mixing bowl. Place the ball of dough in the bowl, and turn it over several times to coat it

completely with a thin layer of butter. Cover the bowl with a kitchen towel, and set it aside in a draft-free spot in the kitchen, or an unheated oven, until it doubles in bulk, about 1½ hours.

6. Butter the bottom and sides of two 8-inch round cake pans. Punch the dough down, and knead it for a minute or two. Divide it in half, and shape each half into a smooth round. Place the rounds in the cake pans.

7. With a pastry brush, gently paint the exposed surface of the dough with the egg. Let the bread rise in a draft-free place until it has doubled in size, about 30 to 40 minutes.

1 egg, well beaten

8. Preheat the oven to 350 degrees.

9. Bake the bread for 30 to 40 minutes, or until the top is a shiny dark brown and the bread sounds hollow when tapped. Turn the loaves out on racks to cool.

Makes 2 round loaves

JENNY JESSOP'S SIX-GRAIN BREAD

On one of my first visits to New England, I had the occasion to visit the mother of a friend of mine who lived in Manchester-by-the-Sea on Cape Ann, just north of Boston. She had a wonderful old house with wide floorboards, original Sandwich glass windows and a staircase to the second floor so steep that only a cat was comfortable climbing it. A large fireplace dominated her kitchen, and she kept it lit on all but the hottest days of summer. But my favorite recollection of this lovely lady was not the warmth of her house or hearth, but the fragrances emanating from her ovens, particularly when they were filled with her baking bread. The recipe that follows is an adaptation of one of her standbys, unusual for its time in its innovative use of several grains.

Preparation time: about 3 hours

1. In a mixing bowl, combine the honey with the water, and stir until the honey is dissolved. Sprinkle the yeast over the water, and allow it to proof. If the yeast is not bubbling at the end of 10 minutes, discard the mixture and repeat the process using fresh yeast.

½ cup honey
⅔ cup lukewarm water
2 tablespoons dry yeast

6 to 7 cups white flour
2 cups whole-wheat flour
1 1/2 cups cracked wheat
1 tablespoon salt

1/2 cup vegetable oil
2 cups lukewarm water

1/2 cup sesame seeds
1/2 cup poppy seeds
1 cup pumpkin or sunflower
    seeds

1 egg, well beaten
2 tablespoons light cream

2. Place 6 cups white flour, the whole wheat flour, the cracked wheat and the salt in a large mixing bowl. Stir them until they are well combined.

3. When the yeast has proofed, stir the vegetable oil and the additional 2 cups water into the yeast mixture, and mix well. Pour the liquid ingredients over the flours, and beat vigorously for 5 minutes, until a sticky dough has formed. Turn the dough out onto a floured surface. Knead it for 10 minutes, gradually incorporating some or all of the remaining 1 cup white flour, until the dough is smooth and elastic.

4. Generously butter a large mixing bowl. Place the ball of dough in the bowl, and turn it over several times to coat it completely with the butter. Cover the bowl with a kitchen towel, and set it aside in a draft-free spot, or an unheated oven, until it doubles in bulk, about 1 hour.

5. Butter the bottom and sides of four 5-by-7-inch loaf pans.

6. Place the seeds together in a pile on a kitchen counter, and, with your fingers or a spoon, mix them briefly. Punch down the dough, knead it once or twice, then place it on top of the seeds. Knead the seeds into the dough until they are well distributed. (This is somewhat arduous because the seeds will resist being absorbed by the dough, but persevere. Eventually they *will* be absorbed.) Divide the dough into four equal parts, and shape the pieces into loaves. Place the loaves in the four loaf pans.

7. In a small bowl, mix the egg into the cream. With a pastry brush, gently paint the exposed surface of the dough with the egg wash. Let the dough rise in a draft-free place until it has doubled in size, about 30 to 40 minutes.

8. Preheat the oven to 350 degrees.

9. Bake the bread for 45 to 50 minutes, or until the top is a shiny brown and the bread sounds hollow when tapped. Turn the loaves out on racks to cool.

Makes 4 loaves

CRANBERRY-APPLE MUFFINS

New Englanders tend to think of their climate as needlessly perverse. "If you don't like the weather here," the old saying goes, "just wait five minutes. It'll change." Sometimes, though, the seasons bring serendipitous combinations of fruits and vegetables to their peak at the same time, and few are more appealing than apples and cranberries.

Just when the cranberry growers are beginning to think about harvesting their bogs, the apple crop comes into its own. Around Columbus Day weekend, hordes of New Englanders and visitors alike travel the back roads of central Massachusetts, Vermont and New Hampshire to pick apples in the orchards, stock up on just-pressed cider and lunch on hot apple dumplings made at roadside stands. And when they get home with their baskets and bags, they head for the kitchen.

Preparation time: about 45 minutes

1. Preheat the oven to 400 degrees. Generously butter one or two (2½-inch) muffin tins.

2. In a strainer, sift together the flour, baking powder, sugar and salt into a bowl.

2 cups flour
2 teaspoons baking powder
¼ cup sugar
½ teaspoon salt

3. In a small bowl, whisk the cooled butter together with the egg, buttermilk and cider. Add the mixture to the dry ingredients, stirring only enough to mix. Do not overbeat. The batter should be stiff.

3 tablespoons unsalted butter, melted and cooled
1 egg, beaten
½ cup buttermilk
½ cup apple cider

4. Fold the cranberries and apple into the batter. Fill the muffin cups two-thirds full with the batter. Sprinkle 1 teaspoon sugar evenly over each muffin.

1 cup coarsely chopped cranberries
1 cup (about 1 large) chopped, cored and peeled apple
½ cup sugar

5. Bake for 20 to 25 minutes, or until a toothpick inserted into the center of a muffin comes out clean. Turn out the muffins on a rack to cool.

Makes about 10 (2¹/₂-inch) muffins

OATMEAL AND PUMPKIN MUFFINS

Preparation time: about 45 minutes

1. Preheat the oven to 400 degrees. Generously butter one or two (2¹/₂-inch) muffin tins.

1 cup "old-fashioned" (thick) rolled oats
1 cup whole wheat flour
¹/₂ cup white flour
2 teaspoons baking powder
¹/₂ teaspoon salt

2. In a large bowl, thoroughly combine the oats, whole-wheat and white flours, baking powder and salt.

2 eggs
³/₄ cup dark brown sugar
¹/₂ cup milk
¹/₄ cup unsalted butter, melted
¹/₂ cup Pumpkin Puree (see p. 178) or canned pumpkin
1 teaspoon vanilla

3. In another bowl, whisk the eggs vigorously with the sugar until they are well mixed. Add the milk, melted butter, pumpkin puree and vanilla, and stir. Pour the mixture over the dry ingredients. With a rubber spatula, fold in the liquid until the dry ingredients are just moistened.

4. Fill the muffin tins two-thirds full with the batter. Bake 20 to 25 minutes, or until the muffins are springy to the touch and a straw inserted in the center of a muffin comes out clean. Turn out the muffins on a rack to cool.

Makes 16 (2¹/₂-inch) muffins

Steaming giant popovers in cloth-covered bread baskets arrive almost as soon as the menus in some New England restaurants. Their light, airy texture invites continuous munching right up to dessert. For successful popovers, preheat both the oven and the tins. The steam given off by the egg-rich batter will expand rapidly, causing the popovers to swell internally and "pop over" the rims of the muffin cups, thus acquiring their characteristic free-form shapes.

Preparation time: about 45 minutes

1. Preheat the oven to 450 degrees. Generously butter one or two popover or muffin tins. Place them in the oven to preheat while you make the batter.

2. In a mixing bowl or blender, combine the milk and eggs, and mix well. Add the flour, salt and sugar (if desired), and mix until the ingredients are just combined.

3. Carefully pour the batter into the hot, buttered tins, filling each cup one-third full. Bake at 450 degrees for 15 minutes, or until the popovers have swelled over the rims of the cups. Reduce the heat to 350 degrees, and continue baking for 20 to 25 minutes, or until the popovers are golden brown. Serve immediately, hot from the oven.

1 cup milk
3 eggs, well beaten
1 cup flour
$1/2$ teaspoon salt
2 teaspoons sugar (optional)

Makes 12 popovers

DOUBLE BLUEBERRY MUFFINS

These muffins—so sweet and delicate they can almost be served for dessert—are best made with wild blueberries, simply because wild berries are smaller than the cultivated kind and don't sink to the bottom. But the real secret of this recipe's success is not the type or quality of the berry, but the fact that the berries' presence is intensified by the cooked blueberry juice.

Preparation time: about 45 minutes

1/4 cup sugar
1/2 cup blueberries
  (preferably wild), washed
  and picked over
1/3 cup milk

1/2 cup unsalted butter,
  softened
1 cup sugar
2 eggs

2 cups cake flour
2 teaspoons baking powder
1/2 teaspoon salt
1/4 teaspoon cinnamon

2 cups blueberries
  (preferably wild), washed
  and picked over

1. Preheat the oven to 425 degrees. Generously butter one or two (2½-inch) muffin tins.

2. In a small saucepan, combine the sugar with the blueberries. Over low heat, bring the berries to a boil, stirring constantly. Boil for 2 minutes; then remove the pan from the heat. Mix in the milk, and set the mixture aside to cool.

3. In a mixing bowl, cream the butter with the sugar until the mixture is light and fluffy. Beat in the eggs, one at a time.

4. Combine the flour, baking powder, salt and cinnamon in a strainer, and sift them together into a bowl.

5. Alternating with the blueberry mixture, add the flour to the butter in three parts, each time beating until the batter is smooth.

6. Gently fold in the blueberries, taking care not to break them. Fill the muffin tins two-thirds full with the batter. Place the tins in the oven, and bake about 20 minutes, or until the muffins are just golden and a straw inserted into the center of a muffin comes out clean. Let the muffins cool in the tins before removing them.

Makes 18 (2½-inch) muffins

HONEY-WHEAT GEMS

At many of New England's famous country inns, a particularly inviting custom is the breakfast basket overflowing with a variety of fresh-baked muffins. Honey-Wheat Gems take their name from a small muffin long popular in Plymouth County, but their use of whole wheat and honey instead of sugar will appeal to today's health-conscious bakers.

Preparation time: about 45 minutes

1. Preheat the oven to 400 degrees. Generously butter one or two (2½-inch) muffin tins.

2. In a strainer, sift together the white and whole-wheat flours, baking powder and salt into a large mixing bowl.

1 cup white flour
1 cup whole-wheat flour
1 tablespoon baking powder
1/4 teaspoon salt

3. In a separate bowl, beat together the egg, buttermilk, honey and butter. Add the liquid to the dry ingredients, and mix until they are well blended. Do not overbeat.

1 egg, beaten
3/4 cup buttermilk
1/4 cup honey
3 tablespoons unsalted butter, melted

4. Fill the muffin tins two-thirds full with the batter, and bake for 20 to 25 minutes, or until a toothpick inserted in the center of a muffin comes out clean. Turn out the muffins on a rack to cool.

Makes 12 (2 1/2-inch) muffins

SQUASH MUFFINS

Preparation time: about 45 minutes

1. Preheat the oven to 400 degrees. Generously butter one or two (2 1/2 inch) muffin tins.

2. In a large bowl, sift together the flour, sugar, baking powder and salt.

1 1/2 cups flour
1/2 cup sugar
2 teaspoons baking powder
1/4 teaspoon salt

3. In another bowl, stir together the egg, milk, butter and squash until they are well blended. Pour them over the dry ingredients, and stir until the batter is just mixed. Do not overbeat.

1 egg, beaten
3/4 cup milk
1 tablespoon unsalted butter, melted
1/2 cup pureed cooked winter squash (or Pumpkin Puree, p. 178)

4. Fill the muffin tins two-thirds full with the batter, and bake for 25 to 30 minutes, or until a toothpick inserted in the center of a muffin comes out clean. Turn out the muffins on a rack to cool.

Makes 9 (2 1/2-inch) muffins

VI

Soups and Chowders

NEW ENGLAND CLAM CHOWDER

New Englanders are an independent lot, set in their own ways. The recipe for clam chowder, New England style—as opposed to tomato-based Manhattan chowder—is pretty standard, except for the type of clams. Over this there are arguments and heated discussion. Some people like to make their chowder with soft-shell (or steamer) clams, some with hard-shell clams (also known as quahogs) and some even with sea clams. We have chosen to make ours with steamers, clams with a delicate flavor and rather long, black necks. Feel free to substitute quahogs (use the 3-inch-long cherrystone variety) or sea clams. They will make the chowder clammier but equally good.

Preparation time: about ³/₄ hour

2 pounds soft-shell, steamer
  clams, well scrubbed (or
  3 dozen cherrystone
  clams)
1 cup water

1. Place the clams in a 3- or 4-quart saucepan. Add the water. Set the pan over high heat, cover, and steam the clams for approximately 10 minutes, or until the shells are open wide. (Discard any that have remained shut.) With a slotted spoon, transfer the clams to a platter to cool. Pour the broth remaining in the saucepan through a strainer lined with a dampened dish towel, catching the broth in a bowl. Reserve 1¹/₂ cups of the clam broth.

When the clams are cool enough to handle, remove them from their shells, and cut off and discard the black necks. Squeeze out and discard the black centers. Chop the clams coarsely, and reserve them. (If you are using cherrystone clams, follow the same procedure but do not concern yourself about discarding necks or centers.)

2. Place the potatoes in a saucepan, cover them with water and bring the water to a boil. Lower the heat, and cook over moderate heat until the potatoes are just tender, about 10 minutes. Drain and reserve them.

1 pound (about 2 large) potatoes, peeled and cut in 1/2-inch cubes

3. In a 3- to 4-quart saucepan, over low heat, sauté the salt pork cubes until they are golden and the fat is rendered. With a slotted spoon, remove the cubes to paper towelling to drain. Reserve them.

2 ounces salt pork, rind removed, cut in 1/4-inch cubes

4. Pour off all but 2 tablespoons of the rendered fat. Add the onion and sauté it, over low heat, until it is wilted, about 5 minutes. Stir in the reserved clam broth, clams and potatoes. Cook over low heat, covered, for 10 minutes.

1 cup finely chopped onion

5. Add the milk and cream, stirring to blend well. Season with salt and pepper. Bring the chowder to just under a boil. Immediately pour it into preheated bowls.

2 cups milk
1/2 cup heavy cream
Salt and freshly ground pepper to taste

6. Float a teaspoon of butter in each bowl, and add a sprinkling of the reserved salt pork cubes on top. Serve.

4 to 6 teaspoons unsalted butter

Makes 8 cups

NEW ENGLAND FISH CHOWDER

New York and New England may argue about what's "real" clam chowder, but there's no debate about fish chowder. A proper fish chowder should be a simple dish of fish, potatoes and a few seasonings in a white broth with perhaps just a bit of yellow from the melted butter floating on top. It should be milky in consistency (although some cooks prefer a higher ratio of cream to milk), and should never, *ever* taste of flour, which is sometimes—mistakenly—used as a thickener. Fish chowder makes a pleasant lunch with salad, or a hearty supper served with crusty bread.

Preparation time: about 1½ hours

¼ *pound salt pork, rind removed, cut in ¼-inch cubes*
1 *cup chopped onion*

1. In a 4- to 6-quart pot, sauté the salt pork cubes over low heat until they are golden and the fat has been rendered. Remove the cubes with a slotted spoon, and reserve them on paper towels. Add the onion to the fat, and cook it, stirring, until it is soft and golden.

2 *pounds cod or haddock fillets, skinned and cut in 1½-inch chunks*
2 *medium potatoes (about 1 pound), peeled and cut into ½-inch cubes*
1 *bay leaf*
1 *teaspoon salt*

2. Add the fish, potatoes, bay leaf and salt to the onion, and cover the ingredients with water. Bring the water to a boil. Reduce the heat and simmer, covered, 10 to 15 minutes, until the potatoes are just tender. Skim off any foam or scum.

2 *cups milk*
2 *cups light cream*
2 *tablespoons unsalted butter*
1 *teaspoon minced fresh thyme (or ¼ teaspoon dried)*

3. Pour the milk and cream into the pot, add the butter and thyme, and stir to blend. Return the chowder to a boil, lower the heat, cover and simmer, stirring occasionally, for 15 minutes.

Freshly ground black pepper to taste

4. Remove and discard the bay leaf. Taste the chowder, and adjust the seasoning, adding pepper to taste.

Vermont Common Crackers or oyster biscuits

5. The chowder may be served immediately or held, refrigerated—which allows its flavors to develop—and reheated. Serve it in heated bowls, with a sprinkling of the reserved salt pork cubes on top, accompanied by Vermont Common Crackers or oyster biscuits.

Makes about 12 cups

RICH LOBSTER CHOWDER

Although chowders are usually considered simple dishes, with just a little extra effort they can become truly elegant. This lobster chowder—devised by a native New Yorker with a sophisticated palate who, while summering in Maine, likes to consume as many of the local lobsters as humanly possible—is rich and golden, thanks to the combination of cream, tomalley (the lobster's liver), egg yolks and sherry.

Preparation time: about 2¹/₄ hours

1. Pour 1 inch of water into a large pot. Bring the water to a boil, and plunge the lobsters, head first, into it. Quickly cover the pot, and steam the lobsters about 15 to 20 minutes, or until one of the small legs can easily be pulled off. Using tongs, remove the lobsters, and allow them to cool.

2 live female lobsters, about 4 pounds total

2. When the lobsters are cool enough to handle, remove the meat from the tails and claws. Remove and reserve the green tomalley and coral-colored roe as well. Reserve the shells.

3. With a cleaver, chop all the lobster shells, including the body, into 2-inch pieces. Place the pieces in a 4- to 5-quart pot. Add the wine, cream, milk, onion, parsley, bay leaf, cloves and peppercorns. Bring the mixture to a simmer over moderate heat. Reduce the heat to low, and simmer, partially covered, about 45 minutes, or until the liquid has thickened slightly and taken on the flavor of the lobster and spices.

2 cups dry white wine
2 cups light cream
2 cups milk
¹/₂ cup finely sliced onion
4 sprigs parsley
1 bay leaf
¹/₄ teaspoon ground cloves
6 whole peppercorns

4. While the broth is simmering, cut the reserved lobster meat into ¹/₂-inch pieces, and set the pieces aside.

5. In a small bowl, using a wooden spoon, cream together the reserved lobster tomalley, roe, cracker crumbs and softened butter.

4 unsalted soda crackers (such as Bremem Wafers), crushed
2 tablespoons unsalted butter, softened

2 egg yolks, well beaten
2 tablespoons dry sherry
1/2 teaspoon salt
Freshly ground black pepper
   to taste

6. In another bowl, whisk together the egg yolks, sherry, salt and pepper.

7. Strain the lobster broth through a sieve lined with a double thickness of cheesecloth into a bowl. Transfer all but 1/4 cup of the broth to the pot, and discard the shells and seasonings. Add the 1/4 cup lobster broth to the tomalley paste, and mix well. Slowly add the moistened tomalley paste and the egg mixture to the pot, beating constantly. Drop in the lobster meat, and simmer over low heat, uncovered, about 10 minutes, or until the meat is thoroughly warmed. Do not allow the chowder to come to a boil, or it will curdle. Taste, and adjust the seasonings.

Paprika
Vermont Common Crackers

8. Serve the chowder immediately in heated bowls with a dusting of paprika for garnish. Accompany the chowder with Vermont Common Crackers.

Makes about 12 cups

CHICKEN AND CORN CHOWDER

Although this chowder is best made with fresh corn, if you're feeling lazy or the corn doesn't look very good, don't feel guilty about resorting to frozen.

Preparation time: about 1 hour

1 pound boned, skinned
   chicken breasts
3 cups water

1. Place the chicken breasts in a 10-inch skillet, cover them with water and bring the water to a boil. Lower the heat, cover the pan and simmer 10 to 15 minutes, depending on the size of the breasts. Transfer the breasts to a plate to cool, and reserve the cooking liquid. When the breasts are cool enough to handle, cut them into 1/2-inch cubes, and reserve the cubes.

4 cups fresh corn kernels
   (from 4 large ears of
   corn), or 2 (10-ounce)
   packages frozen corn
   kernels, thawed

2. In a food processor fitted with a steel blade, puree 2 cups of the corn until smooth, scraping the bowl occasionally with a rubber spatula. (Or puree the corn in a food mill.) Reserve the puree along with the remaining 2 cups corn.

3. With a sharp knife, starting from ½ inch above the root end, cut each leek lengthwise down the middle. (Do not cut all the way through to the root end.) Rinse the leeks under cold water, spreading the leaves apart to dislodge any grit. Shake well to remove excess water. Cut the leeks crosswise into thin slices. There should be approximately 2 cups. (Or substitute 2 cups chopped sweet onion, such as Vidalia.)

4. In a 3- to 4-quart saucepan, over low heat, render the fat from the salt pork. Cook the bits, turning them frequently, until they are golden. With a slotted spoon, remove and discard the cubes. To the fat remaining in the pan, add the leeks and celery, and sauté them over low heat until they are soft, about 10 minutes.

5. Add the cubed potatoes, the reserved chicken broth and cubed chicken, the chicken stock, the pureed corn, and the whole corn kernels to the saucepan. Mix well. Bring the mixture to a boil over high heat, stirring frequently; then lower the heat and simmer, partially covered, for 15 minutes or until the potatoes are tender. Stir in the cream, and continue to simmer for 5 more minutes. Add salt and pepper.

6. Ladle the chowder into preheated soup bowls, and sprinkle with chives.

Makes 10 cups

2 large leeks, trimmed of roots and green leaves

2 ounces salt pork, rind removed, cut in ¼-inch cubes
1 cup chopped celery

1 pound (about 2 large) potatoes, peeled and cut in ½-inch cubes
2 cups chicken stock, preferably homemade
1 cup heavy cream
Salt and freshly ground pepper to taste

3 tablespoons minced fresh chives

CORN CHOWDER

Every now and then, New England's shores will be whipped by a "Nor'Easter," a three-day blast of wind and rain. Damp permeates homes, and chill penetrates even the most well-insulated bones. These are true Soup Days. In August, one of the most satisfying soups for the occasion is Corn Chowder, made from freshly gathered local corn.

Preparation time: about ¾ hour

4 cups fresh corn kernels, (from 4 large ears of corn), or 2 (10-ounce) packages frozen corn kernels, thawed

1. Place 2 cups of the corn in a food processor fitted with a steel blade. Puree the corn until it is smooth, scraping the bowl occasionally with a rubber spatula. (Or puree the corn in a food mill.) Reserve the puree along with the remaining 2 cups corn.

2 ounces salt pork, rind removed, cut in 1/4-inch cubes

2. In a 3- to 4-quart saucepan, over low heat, render the fat from the salt pork. Cook the bits, turning them frequently, until they are golden. With a slotted spoon, transfer the pork bits to paper towelling to drain. Reserve them.

1 large onion (about 1 pound), cut in half crosswise, each half thinly sliced
1 pound (about 2 large) potatoes, peeled and cut into 1/4-inch cubes
2 cups chicken stock, preferably homemade
2 cups milk

3. In the fat remaining in the saucepan, sauté the sliced onion over moderate heat, stirring frequently, until it is wilted, about 10 minutes. Add the reserved corn puree, the remaining 2 cups of corn kernels, the potatoes, the chicken stock and the milk. Stir well to blend the ingredients. Bring to a boil over high heat, reduce the heat to low and simmer, covered, for 15 minutes, or until the potatoes are tender.

1 cup sour cream or yogurt
Salt and freshly ground pepper to taste

4. Remove the pan from the heat, and add the sour cream or yogurt. With a whisk, beat until it is completely assimilated. Add salt and pepper. Return the chowder to a moderate heat, and cook it about 5 minutes longer, stirring frequently, to bring it just under a boil. Do not allow the chowder to boil.

5. Immediately ladle the chowder into preheated soup bowls, and sprinkle the surface with the reserved pork bits.

Makes 12 cups

MUSSEL AND SCALLOP CHOWDER

With its multitude of bays and inlets, islands and barrier beaches, New England's coastline is more than six thousand miles long, or almost double the width of the United States. No wonder, then, we have an abundance of fish and shellfish literally at our fingertips. One of the great joys of living near the seashore is being able to partake of the sea's harvests. Mussels are among the easiest to obtain; they grow in great profusion, and they lie, for the grabbing, right underwater if the bottom is sandy, or else, if the coast is rocky, they cling tenaciously to any outcrop. Delicately flavored bay scallops are available only at certain seasons, but the larger sea scallops, nearly as good, are available year-round—as are mussels. This recipe is a lovely melding of two favorite sea-rich flavors.

Preparation time: about 3/4 hour

1. Pour the water into a 3- to 4-quart saucepan. Add the mussels. Cover the saucepan, and bring the water to a boil. When the lid starts rising with the steam, lower the heat. Continue to cook the mussels, partially covered, for 5 to 8 minutes, or until their shells have opened. Set the mussels aside, still in the pot, to cool. When they can be handled, remove the meat from the shells. If the mussels are extremely large, cut them in half crosswise; otherwise leave them whole. Reserve the meat in a separate dish, and discard the shells. Discard any mussels whose shells have not opened. Line a strainer with a double thickness of dampened cheesecloth or a moistened linen towel, and pour the broth through it. Reserve 1 cup broth.

2 cups water
1 1/2 pounds mussels, well scrubbed, "beards" pulled off

2. While the mussels are cooking, drop the potato into boiling salted water. Cook it for 15 minutes, or until it is tender. Drain and reserve it.

1 medium potato (about 1/2 pound), peeled and cut in 1/2-inch cubes

3. Melt the butter in a 3- to 4-quart saucepan over moderate heat. Add the onions, lower the heat, and cook until the onions are soft, about 5 minutes. Drop in the scallops, increase the heat to moderate, and cook them, stirring frequently, for 1 minute, or until they turn opaque. Add the reserved cup of mussel broth, bring it to a boil, lower the heat, and cook 2 minutes longer. Add the potato and mussels. Finally, pour in the milk and cream, stir to blend well, and season with salt and pepper. Bring the chowder to just under a boil.

3 tablespoons unsalted butter
1 cup chopped onions
1 pound sea scallops
2 1/2 cups milk
1/2 cup heavy cream
Salt and freshly ground pepper to taste

4. Ladle the hot chowder into preheated soup bowls, and sprinkle with coriander or chives.

3 tablespoons minced fresh cilantro or chives

Makes 6 cups

MILLIE'S HAM AND BEAN SOUP

Millie was a friend and neighbor who lived on Cape Cod. She used to make the best bean soup, which she would carry out to the beach as her contribution to our Fourth of July picnic. She never followed a recipe, so the soup never tasted quite the same twice. But it was always wonderful. This is my reconstruction of one version of Millie's memorable soup.

Preparation time: about 3 hours

1 pound navy beans,
* washed and picked over*

1. Pour the beans into a 4- to 6-quart stockpot, and cover them with 2 inches of water. Bring the water to a boil, and boil for 3 minutes. Turn off the heat, and let the beans soak for 1 hour.

1 medium onion, peeled
4 cloves
2 bay leaves
6 sprigs parsley
1 teaspoon thyme
1 teaspoon salt

2. Pierce the onion with the cloves. Make a bouquet garni by combining the bay leaves, parsley and thyme in a cheesecloth bag, tied tightly with string. Add the onion and the herbs to the beans, along with the salt, and stir to mix. Add more water (if needed) to cover the beans by 1 inch. Bring to a boil again, lower the heat, and simmer, partially covered, for 30 to 60 minutes, or until the beans are tender but not mushy. Discard the onion and the bouquet garni. Drain the beans through a sieve, catching the cooking liquid in a bowl. There should be at least 1½ cups liquid; if not, add water to make this amount. Reserve the liquid. Return the beans to the stockpot, and reserve them off the stove.

4 tablespoons unsalted
* butter*
1 tablespoon minced garlic
1½ cups chopped onion
1 cup chopped celery
1 cup chopped carrots

3. Melt the butter in a large skillet. Add the garlic, onion and celery, and sauté over low heat, stirring occasionally, until the vegetables are wilted, about 10 minutes. Add the carrots and the reserved 1½ cups bean broth, bring to a boil, and cook over moderate heat for 10 minutes.

4. With a rubber spatula, scrape the onion mixture into the reserved beans. Add the tomatoes, ham cubes and chicken stock. Mix well. Bring the soup slowly to a boil over moderate heat, stirring frequently. Taste, and season with salt and pepper. Ladle the soup into preheated soup bowls, and garnish with a sprinkling of minced parsley.

1 (28-ounce) can crushed peeled tomatoes
1 pound ham steak, trimmed of fat, cut in ¹/₂-inch cubes
6 cups chicken stock, preferably homemade
Salt and freshly ground pepper to taste
¹/₂ cup minced parsley

Makes 16 cups

CREAM OF BLACK BEAN SOUP

Here's a more elegant version of Millie's Ham and Bean Soup, this time made with black beans. (If you can't find them in your supermarket, try a Hispanic market.) The black beans give the finished soup an unusual but attractive purplish color, and bits of ham and pureed bean create a speckled effect, as well as adding texture.

Preparation time: about 3¹/₂ hours

1. Wash and pick over the dried beans. Place them in a 3- to 4-quart pot, and cover them with water by 2 inches. Bring the water to a boil, and boil 3 minutes. Turn off the heat, and allow the beans to soak for 1 hour.

1 pound black turtle beans

2. Drain the beans, and return them to the pot. Cover them with fresh water, and add the ham. Bring the water to a boil; then reduce the heat and simmer, covered, about 2 hours, or until the beans are tender. About 15 minutes before the beans are cooked, remove the ham and set it aside to cool.

1 (1- to 1¹/₂-pound) ham steak, cut in quarters

3. When the ham is cool enough to handle, remove any fat and bone, and discard them. Mince the meat, and place it in a large pot. Place a colander over the same pot, and drain the beans over it, allowing the broth to run through.

4. In a food processor with a steel blade, or in a blender or food mill, puree the beans to a thick paste. (This may have to be done in

batches.) Add the puree to the soup pot, and begin to reheat the soup over moderate heat, stirring occasionally to break up the puree.

4 tablespoons unsalted
  butter
4 tablespoons flour
1 small onion, minced
1/4 teaspoon freshly ground
  black pepper
1/4 teaspoon dry mustard
2 cups light cream
Salt and freshly ground
  pepper to taste

5. While the soup heats, melt the butter in a 1-quart saucepan. Gradually add the flour, stirring to break up any lumps. Add the onion, pepper, mustard powder and cream. Stir and warm the mixture gently, uncovered, until it has thickened slightly.

6. Add the cream mixture to the soup pot. Stir and simmer the ingredients together until they are heated through; do not allow soup to boil. Taste, and season with salt and pepper.

3 hard-boiled eggs, finely
  chopped
1/4 cup minced parsley

7. Ladle the soup into heated bowls. Sprinkle with the chopped egg and parsley to garnish.

Makes about 16 cups

PORTUGUESE KALE SOUP

This is a wonderfully hearty soup, a meal in itself. Serve it in large bowls, accompanied by crisp French or Italian bread, freshly warmed in the oven.

Preparation time: about 1 hour

2 tablespoons vegetable oil
1 1/2 cups finely chopped
  onion
2 teaspoons minced garlic
1 1/2 pounds (about 3 large)
  potatoes, peeled and sliced
  1/4-inch thick
8 cups chicken stock,
  preferably homemade

1. In a large soup pot or flame-proof casserole, warm the oil over moderate heat. Add the onion and garlic; cook, stirring frequently, until they are wilted, about 5 minutes. Add the potato slices and the stock, and bring to a boil. Lower the heat and simmer, partially covered, for 15 minutes or until the potatoes are very tender when pierced with the tip of a knife.

2. Meanwhile, prick the sausage all over with the tines of a fork. Place it in a frying pan, and cover it with water. Bring the water to a boil, reduce the heat to low, and simmer for 15 minutes. Transfer the sausage to paper towelling to drain. When it is cool enough to handle, slice the sausage 1/4-inch thick, and reserve it.

3. In batches, transfer the contents of the soup pot to an electric blender or food processor fitted with a steel blade, and whirl the mixture until it is smooth. Return it to the pot.

4. Add the tomatoes and kidney beans to the potato puree, and stir to blend. Bring the soup to a boil, drop in the strips of kale and reduce the heat to low. Simmer, partially covered, for 25 minutes, stirring occasionally. Add the reserved sausage slices, and simmer 5 minutes longer. Taste, and season with salt and pepper.

5. Serve immediately in heated soup bowls.

1 pound linguica or chourico sausage

1 (28-ounce) can crushed peeled tomatoes
1 (15-ounce) can (1 1/2 cups) kidney beans, drained and rinsed under cold water
3/4 pound fresh kale (or collard greens), washed, drained, stemmed, and cut in 1/4-inch strips
Salt and freshly ground pepper to taste

Makes 12 cups

CURRIED SQUASH SOUP

Native to America, squash has been a New England staple since long before the Pilgrims arrived. Extremely versatile in its many varieties, it is used in New England in every kind of dish from appetizers to desserts. This creamy, slightly curried soup makes a fine first course, but it's hearty enough to stand on its own, accompanied by salad and warm bread.

Preparation time: about 2 1/2 hours

1. Preheat the oven to 350 degrees.

2. Cut the squash in half lengthwise, and scoop out the seeds and strings. Place the halves, cut side down, on a buttered baking dish, and bake them about 30 to 45 minutes, or until they are

2 pounds hubbard or butternut squash

2 tablespoons unsalted
  butter
2 tablespoons curry powder
1/2 cup chopped onion
1/8 teaspoon allspice
1/8 teaspoon ground cloves
1/4 teaspoon ground ginger
1/2 teaspoon salt

2 cups chicken stock,
  preferably homemade
2 cups milk

1 cup heavy cream
3 tablespoons snipped chives

tender when pierced with the tip of a knife. Remove the squash from the oven. When it is barely cool enough to handle, scoop the pulp into a bowl, and reserve it.

3. In a 4- to 5-quart pot, melt the butter over low heat. Add the curry powder and cook, stirring, for 2 to 3 minutes, to release its flavor. Add the onions, and sauté them until they are wilted, about 5 minutes. Mix in the allspice, cloves, ginger and salt. Add the squash pulp, mashing it with a wooden spoon to break up the larger lumps. Slowly pour in the chicken stock and milk, and, stirring constantly, bring the mixture to a boil. Reduce the heat and simmer, uncovered, 15 minutes.

4. Remove the pot from the heat, and allow the soup to cool slightly. In batches, transfer it to a blender or the bowl of a food processor fitted with a steel blade, and puree the soup until it is smooth.

5. The soup may be served hot or cold. To serve it hot, return the pureed soup to the pot, and stir in the cream, mixing until it is well blended in. Slowly reheat the soup to just under the boiling point. Serve it immediately, garnished with chives. To serve it cold, transfer the pureed soup to a large bowl, blend in the cream and refrigerate the soup until it is thoroughly chilled. Garnish with chives.

Makes about 14 cups

VII

Fish and Shellfish

Lobster

Today, partly because of their subtle flavor and partly because of their exorbitant prices, we consider lobsters a delicacy. The Pilgrims, in contrast, fed them to their pigs. Undoubtedly the reason was the overwhelming abundance of lobsters in New England waters in the seventeenth century. When the Pilgrims arrived, lobsters swarmed not only in Plymouth Harbor but throughout Cape Cod Bay, and they were giants, many measuring 4 to 6 feet long. (Lobsters continue growing until they die. For some years the New England Aquarium in Boston has had a live 40-pounder in its collection.) The sweet, rich meat of a lobster will taste good with just about any preparation. There's nothing finer in a New England summer than a lobster consumed outdoors, simply steamed or boiled or baked, enhanced only by a squeeze of fresh lemon and a dip into drawn butter. But this crustacean's dramatic appearance easily lends itself to more elaborate presentations, such as Lobster Newburg, Thermidor or Savannah.

Sadly, many visitors to New England miss the experience of eating a whole lobster because they're intimidated by the prospect of dismembering it armed only with a nutcracker, a pick and their bare hands. Actually, eating a whole lobster is a simple matter, if a little messy. The claws should be twisted off the body and cracked with the nutcracker. The tail, too, should be twisted off and cracked open, if it has not already been split, and the meat can usually be pulled out in one or two large pieces. Also edible are the greenish liver, or tomalley, near the top of the tail and, in female lobsters, the coral-colored roe. The gelatinous stomach sac and the intestinal vein running down the tail should be discarded.

STEAMED LOBSTER

Steaming is a good, basic way of cooking lobsters. Although some people prefer to boil them in a deep kettle, steaming them in just an inch or two of water not only takes less time but also leaves the meat more flavorful and juicy.

Preparation time: about 30 minutes

1 (1- to 3-pound) live
   lobster per person
Sea water (or salted fresh
   water)

1. Into a large pot with a tight-fitting lid, pour about 2 inches of sea water. Cover the pot, and bring the water to a full, rolling boil. Drop the live lobsters head first into the pot as quickly as possible. Cover the pot immediately.

2. When the water returns to a rapid boil, steam the lobsters, allowing 12 minutes for 1-pounders, 15 to 18 minutes for 1½-pounders, 20 to 22 minutes for 2-pounders, and 30 to 35 minutes for 3-pounders. To test for doneness, remove one lobster from the pot with tongs, holding it by one of the small legs. Give it a shake. If the leg pulls off, the lobster is done. If not, continue steaming until it does.

3. Using tongs, remove the lobsters from the pot. Serve them immediately with lemon wedges and plenty of drawn butter; or allow the lobsters to cool, remove the meat and reserve it for another preparation.

LOCKE-OBER'S LOBSTER SAVANNAH

Locke-Ober's is a famous Boston restaurant and landmark that opened in 1879.

Preparation time: about 1 1/2 hours

1. Prepare the lobsters for boiling: With short pieces of string, tie wooden spoons or dowels onto their backs to form spines so that the tails will not curl during cooking. Using the widest pot available so that the lobsters will lie flat, follow the basic directions for Steamed Lobster on page 78. When the lobsters are done, remove them from the pot using tongs, cut off the strings and stop the cooking process by rinsing the lobsters under cold water. (If a tail has curved, straighten it and weigh it down with a small cutting board or heavy pan until it holds its shape.) Allow the lobsters to cool until you can handle them comfortably.

2. Remove the claws by twisting them off close to the body. Using a nutcracker and a pick or small fork, remove the claw meat. Set the meat aside. Remove the antennae and discard them, along with the claw shells.

3. Using a sharp knife or kitchen scissors, cut a long oval 1 1/2 to 2 inches wide down the back of each lobster shell, from the back of the head to the point just before the tail fans out. (Work carefully; lobster shells cut the skin easily.) Pull out the tail meat, cut it into 1/2-inch chunks, and add it to the claw meat. Remove any coral-colored roe or green tomalley, and reserve it. Remove the gelatinous stomach sac and the intestinal vein down the tail, and discard them. (The lobsters may be prepared to this point up to 24 hours in advance. Wrap them tightly and refrigerate them.)

4. If the lobsters have been refrigerated, bring them to room temperature. One-half hour before serving, preheat the oven to 400 degrees. In a large, heavy skillet over medium-low heat, melt the butter. Add the mushroom slices and green pepper, and sauté them for about 5 minutes, until they are just soft.

5. Stir the flour into the mushrooms and pepper, and mix well. Let it cook for about 1 minute, stirring constantly. Slowly add the milk and, whisking constantly, bring the sauce to a boil. Reduce the heat to low, and stir in any tomalley and roe, the sherry, paprika, salt and pepper. Simmer about 5 minutes. Add the pimiento and the lobster meat, and stir until they are coated with sauce. Taste, and adjust the seasonings.

4 (1 1/2-pound) live lobsters
Sea water (or salted fresh water)

3 tablespoons unsalted butter
1/2 cup thinly sliced white mushrooms
1/4 cup finely chopped green pepper

2 tablespoons flour
1 cup milk
1/4 cup dry sherry
1 teaspoon paprika
1 teaspoon salt
Freshly ground black pepper to taste
2 tablespoons pimiento, finely chopped

1/4 cup white bread crumbs,
   preferably homemade
3 tablespoons freshly grated
   parmesan cheese

6. Place the lobster shells on a large baking sheet or jelly roll pan. Remove the lobster mixture from the heat, and spoon it into the shells, dividing it evenly. Mix the bread crumbs and the parmesan cheese, and sprinkle it evenly over the lobster filling.

7. Bake the lobsters about 15 minutes, until the sauce bubbles and the bread crumbs are light brown. Remove them from the oven, and serve them immediately.

Serves 4

LOBSTER SALAD WITH TOMATO MAYONNAISE

Like shrimp and crab, lobster makes a very special salad. New Englanders serve it many ways. Sometimes they mix the meat with a mayonnaise-based dressing; sometimes they arrange it on a bed of greens, offering any number of different dressings as accompaniments. The lobster meat may be finely shredded, forming almost a paste when mixed with the dressing, or left in bite-size chunks.

The chunky style retains more of the sweetness and texture of lobster meat. What's more, it's better in "lobster rolls," the New England sandwich of lobster salad packed into a long, frankfurter style bun. (Similarly, there are shrimp rolls, crab rolls and clam rolls.)

Some of the finest lobster rolls in New England are served just north of Boston at an unpretentious stand on Revere Beach called Kelly's Famous Roast Beef. Kelly's lobster salad definitely falls into the "chunky" category; it's not unusual to bite into a roll and find a small whole tail or claw.

Preparation time: about 1 hour

4 (1 1/2-pound) live lobsters
   (or 2 pounds fresh-cooked
   lobster meat)

1. If you are starting with live lobsters, follow the directions for Steamed Lobster (see p. 78), rinsing the lobster with cold water immediately after cooking. When the lobster is cool enough to handle, remove the tail and claw meat, cut it into 1-inch chunks, and reserve it.

2. Make the tomato mayonnaise: In a food processor with a plastic mixing blade, place the egg yolks, salt and lemon juice. Whirl on medium speed for about 2 minutes, until the mixture is pale yellow. In a large measuring cup with a spout, combine the vegetable and olive oils. Through the feed tube, with the processor running continuously, add the oil drop by drop. Scrape down the sides of the bowl periodically. When half the oil has been added and the mixture has thickened, slowly add the remaining oil in a very thin stream. After all the oil has been incorporated, add the chopped tomatoes with any juices that have accumulated, and whirl until the mayonnaise is well mixed. (Or make the mayonnaise by hand, beating continuously as you add the oil.)

3. In a large bowl, toss the reserved lobster meat and the celery with just enough tomato mayonnaise to coat it. (Reserve leftover mayonnaise for another use.) Add salt and pepper, and toss the salad until it is thoroughly mixed. Serve the lobster salad mounded on lettuce leaves, with tomato slices as garnish if desired, or on toasted frankfurter rolls.

3 egg yolks
¹/₂ teaspoon salt
1¹/₂ teaspoons strained fresh lemon juice
³/₄ cup vegetable oil
¹/₂ cup olive oil
1 pound tomatoes, peeled, seeded and finely chopped

1 cup coarsely chopped celery
Salt and freshly ground pepper to taste
Lettuce leaves (optional)
Fresh tomato slices (optional)
Toasted frankfurter rolls (optional)

Serves 6 to 8

LEEK, CORN AND OYSTER STEW

New England is blessed with an abundance of oysters, of which the best-known varieties are named after their locale, namely the waters off Cotuit and Wellfleet in Massachusetts. True oyster lovers will argue that the only fit way to eat an oyster is raw and freshly opened, on the half shell. Purists will scoff at any sauce, even turning down a sprinkling of lemon juice. But cooked oysters can be praiseworthy as well if two rules are observed. They too must be freshly opened, and they must not be overcooked, which would toughen them. The stew will only be as good as the oysters put into it.

Preparation time: about 30 minutes

2 large leeks, trimmed of roots and green leaves	1. With a sharp knife, starting from ½ inch above the root end, cut each leek lengthwise down the middle. (Do not cut all the way through to the root end.) Rinse the leeks under cold water, spreading the leaves apart to dislodge any grit. Shake well to remove excess water. Cut the leeks crosswise into thin slices. There should be approximately 2 cups.

2 large leeks, trimmed of roots and green leaves

1. With a sharp knife, starting from ½ inch above the root end, cut each leek lengthwise down the middle. (Do not cut all the way through to the root end.) Rinse the leeks under cold water, spreading the leaves apart to dislodge any grit. Shake well to remove excess water. Cut the leeks crosswise into thin slices. There should be approximately 2 cups.

3 tablespoons unsalted butter

2. Melt the butter over moderately low heat in a 3-quart stainless steel saucepan. Add the leeks, stir to coat the pieces with the melted butter, cover the pan and steam them until they are soft, about 8 minutes.

1 (10-ounce) package frozen corn, thawed

3. Add the corn, and stir to mix it with the leeks. Cover the pan and, increasing the heat to moderate, cook the corn for 5 minutes or until it is thoroughly heated.

1 pint freshly shucked oysters, with their liquor

4. Add the oysters and their liquor, and stir to blend them with the vegetables. Cook the oysters over moderate heat, stirring continually, until their edges start to curl, about 3 to 4 minutes.

2 cups light cream
2 cups milk
1 teaspoon salt
Freshly ground black pepper to taste

5. Increase the heat to moderately high. Add the cream and milk, and mix well. Stirring frequently, bring the stew to just under a boil. Remove the pan from the heat. Add the salt and pepper. Serve immediately.

Serves 4

New England Clambakes

Clambakes—those born-in-New-England ultra-special picnic events—are as much a part of our environment as our stretches of white sand beaches, our undulating hills and our boulder-strewn mountains. They are summertime affairs, and they aren't hard to find, whether they're held at the edge of a verdant tidal marsh, at the foot of a massive Atlantic dune, in front of a fire station, on a house-lined village green or right in someone's backyard. No matter the location, there are always crowds around them.

Tradition has it that we inherited the concept of "bakes" from our Native American forebears who, or so the story goes, would celebrate with a fish-and-shellfish feast when they returned to the shore in summertime from their more sheltered domiciles inland.

Unfortunately, no historical documentation has turned up to prove this thesis true. We do know that clambakes reached the zenith of their popularity towards the end of the nineteenth century in the multifaceted coves of Narragansett Bay in Rhode Island. There, a phenomenon known as "Clambake Resorts" erupted. Daily, thousands of tourists sallied forth from the outlying reaches, on foot, buggy, train or even excursion steamer, to gorge themselves on corn and clams, chowder, sausages, chicken, sweet potatoes, hot dogs and, of course, lobster.

Today most clambakes are privately conducted or catered affairs run by "bake masters," as they are called. A large pit is lined with red-hot stones and rockweed—that peculiar green-black seaweed studded with salt water–filled orange bubble-like pods—which is also layered between and on top of the chosen ingredients. Clams are put on the bottom, followed by lobster, chicken or sausage and packets of fish, which are topped with onions and unhusked ears of corn. A dampened tarp, secured by heavy stones, covers the bake to prevent the steam from the rockweed, clams and lobsters from escaping, so that the heat is contained and very intense. The odor emanating from the mound is pungent and hard to resist.

For those for whom the demands of a real clambake are too arduous, here is a mini-stove-top version which, while it may not be traditional, works and tastes almost, if not entirely, as good as the Real Thing.

STOVE-TOP NEW ENGLAND CLAMBAKE

Preparation time: about 1 hour

1. Into a clam-steamer or large kettle (about 20 quarts), pour 1 inch of water. Divide the rockweed or spinach and salt in 4 equal parts. Place one quarter in the bottom of the steamer, and nestle the lobsters on top. Cover the lobsters with another layer of rockweed, and position the corn on it. Cover the corn with a third layer of rockweed, and scatter the clams over it. Cover the clams with the last of the rockweed.

2. Bring the steamer to a boil over high heat, covered, and steam the "bake" for 30 to 45 minutes, or until the clam shells have opened wide.

2 to 3 pounds rockweed (or fresh spinach blended with 4 teaspoons salt)
4 (1½-pound) live lobsters
8 ears of corn, shucked
4 pounds steamer clams, soaked to remove sand

½ pound unsalted butter, melted

3. Divide the lobster, clams and corn between four large platters, and serve with equal portions of melted butter. Discard the rockweed.

Serves 4

QUAHOG PIE

Most everybody—not just New Englanders—loves our native hard-shell clams (*Venus mercenaria*), which we call quahogs (pronounced "co-hogs"). The name is derived from the Algonquian Indian word for clam, *quahaug*. The smaller varieties, cherrystones and littlenecks, are most often consumed raw. Occasionally, though, some little ones escape the clam diggers' rakes and grow up into big ½-pound monster clams, too tough for eating raw. These we always call quahogs, for the word can refer to either the whole species or its largest members only. No self-respecting frugal Yankee would consider dismissing their culinary potential, though, and a number of recipes have evolved over the years utilizing these giant clams to great advantage, among them my family's hands-down favorite, Quahog Pie. (Incidentally, there are as many versions of this recipe as there are clams in our cold waters, some calling for rendered salt pork instead of butter, and flour instead of cracker crumbs. I am simply reproducing here the one we like best. Feel free to make substitutions.) Sea or bar clams may be substituted in this recipe for quahogs.

Preparation time: about 2 hours

15 pounds quahogs (about 30 ½-pound hard-shell clams), well scrubbed

1. Pour about 1 inch of water into a large steaming kettle. Add the clams, cover the pot and bring the liquid to a boil. Steam the clams, turning them occasionally to redistribute them, for approximately 15 minutes, or until all the shells have opened. (Discard any that haven't.) With a slotted spoon, remove the clams to the kitchen sink to cool. Strain the clam juice that has exuded, and reserve ¼ cup for the pie. (Save the rest for other uses.)

2. When the shells are cool enough to handle, remove the clam meat, and transfer it to a bowl. Place the bowl in the freezer, and freeze the clams until they just begin to harden. Do not let them freeze solid.

3. Transfer them to the bowl of a food processor (in batches if necessary), and, pulsating the motor on and off, chop them coarsely. (Or, without freezing the clams first, cut them into pieces with scissors.) You should have about 3 to 4 cups chopped clams. Reserve 3 cups for the Quahog Pie, saving the rest for another use.

4. Preheat the oven to 375 degrees.

5. In a large skillet, melt the butter over moderate heat. Add the onions, and sauté them until they are soft, about 5 minutes. Add the clams and thyme, mix well, and cook over moderately low heat, stirring occasionally, for 10 minutes. Remove the skillet from the heat.

2 tablespoons unsalted butter
3/4 cup coarsely chopped onions
3 cups coarsely chopped quahogs
1 teaspoon thyme

6. Pour the clam juice and cracker crumbs over the clam mixture, and mix well.

1/4 cup clam juice
1/2 cup crumbled crackers, such as Saltines

7. Drop the egg into a small bowl, and beat well. Beat in the cream and parsley. Pour the cream into the clam mixture, and stir to mix thoroughly.

1 egg
1 cup heavy cream
2 tablespoons minced parsley

8. Transfer the quahog filling to a 9½-inch pie plate lined with Flaky Pastry. Cover with a second crust, cutting a few slits in it with a sharp knife to allow steam to escape. Seal the crusts together tightly.

1 recipe Flaky Pie Pastry (see page 183)

9. Bake the pie for 45 to 50 minutes, or until the top crust is lightly browned.

Serves 8

STEAMED CLAMS

One of the greatest joys of a New England summer by the sea is digging for clams, be they the soft-shell (*Mya arenaria*) or hard-shell (*Venus mercenaria*) variety. Soft-shell, long-neck clams are used for steaming, and they are generally found in sandy beds in bays or harbors, their presence identified at low tide by telltale holes in the sand, made by their siphons. Once a clam hole has been spotted, the trick is to start digging, with either fingers or a clam rake, before the prize burrows beyond reach. Clams are particularly vulnerable to pollution and noxious plankton (such as the so-called red tide), so before digging—and one always needs to obtain a local shellfish permit to do so—it is advisable to check with the shellfish warden to make certain the water is pure.

Soft-shell clams, such as steamers, have an annoying habit of ingesting sand, so prior to preparation, they should be soaked for a number of hours until they release their grit. My favorite method is to place them in a container of sea water and let them rest, refrigerated, for 6 to 12 hours. Another popular purging technique is to soak the clams in a salt-water solution (at a ratio of 1/3 cup salt to 1 gallon of water) to which is added 1 cup of cornmeal. Advocates of this method will tell you that the clams will expel their sand and siphon in the meal, thus becoming simultaneously grit-free and fatter. Whichever method you choose, do allow a minimum of 6 hours' soaking time.

It is not easy to estimate the amount of clams needed for each individual, since taste and appetites vary greatly. I generally allow 2 pounds per person, but I have had guests who have consumed 4 pounds apiece. Err on the side of generosity. If you are fortunate enough to have leftovers, you can make any number of dishes, such as clam dip or Linguine with Fresh Clam Sauce (see p. 87).

To eat a steamer clam, remove it from its shell. Pull off and discard the tough outer coating of the black neck. Dip the clam first into the broth and then into the melted butter, and eat it immediately. Discard the shell.

Preparation time: about 6 hours soaking, 15 minutes steaming

1. Into a 6- to 8-quart kettle, pour 1 inch of fresh water. Add the clams, cover the kettle and, over high heat, bring the liquid to a boil. Steam the clams for 5 to 8 minutes, tossing them midway with a slotted spoon. All the shells should have opened. If not, discard those that haven't.

4 pounds soft-shell steamer clams, scrubbed clean and soaked

2. Divide the clams evenly between two heated shallow bowls. Strain the liquid remaining in the kettle through a strainer lined with a double thickness of cheesecloth (or a linen towel) into a bowl. Pour this broth into two cups, and divide the melted butter between two other cups. Serve the broth and melted butter with the clams.

½ cup unsalted butter, melted

Serves 2

LINGUINE WITH FRESH CLAM SAUCE

Many people of Italian heritage live in the area of Boston known as the North End, one of Boston's oldest neighborhoods. (It was here that Paul Revere fashioned his silver and prepared for his famous midnight ride.) Even today the North End has narrow winding streets and three- to four-story brick buildings whose windows seem to burst forth in the summer with a profusion of flower-packed window boxes. It is also home to a plethora of Italian restaurants, some the size of matchboxes, some cavernous, whose well-known "home cooking" attracts hordes of diners. Because of Boston's proximity to the sea, some of their best dishes are seafood-based. One of my favorites, either eaten there or made at home, is pasta sauced with garlic-infused fresh minced clams. If you are using leftover, already cooked steamers, simply chop the clams and cook them only long enough to heat them through, about 2 minutes.

Preparation time: about 20 minutes

1. Pour the olive oil into a large skillet, preferably one with high sides, and set it over moderate heat. When the oil is hot, add 1 to 3 teaspoons garlic, according to your preference. Lower the heat slightly, and, stirring occasionally, sauté the garlic until it is soft, about 5 minutes.

⅓ cup olive oil
1 to 3 teaspoons minced garlic, according to taste

2 cups strained fresh clam
   broth (see page 42)
1/4 cup minced fresh basil
   (or 2 teaspoons dried)
1/2 cup minced parsley
Freshly ground black pepper
   to taste

2. Pour in the clam broth, and stir to mix. Add the basil, parsley and black pepper. (The sauce may be made ahead to this point, and held for final completion.)

2 cups chopped fresh quahog
   clams (see page 84)

4 quarts water
3 tablespoons olive oil
1 tablespoon salt
1 (1-pound) package
   linguine pasta
Freshly grated romano or
   parmesan cheese
   (optional)

3. Add the clams and cook them, over moderate heat, stirring frequently, until they are just done, about 5 minutes. Do not overcook the clams or they will toughen.

4. In a large pot, bring the water to a rolling boil. Add the olive oil and salt. Drop the linguine in, stir vigorously to separate the strands and cook *al dente*, or until barely done, according to the package's directions. Immediately drain the linguine and divide it among 4 heated bowls or plates. Top with the clam sauce, and serve accompanied by grated cheese, if desired.

Serves 4

STEAMED MUSSELS WITH LINGUICA

At long last mussels are being recognized in the United States as the delicacy they are. Maine is the leading producer—and exporter—of these blue-black bivalve mollusks that grow in clusters, attached to one another, on rocks or clumps of seaweed. They are easy to gather, but one word of caution: they should only be taken from free-flowing water below the low-tide level. Mussels may be steamed in much the same manner as Steamed Clams (see p. 86) and dipped in drawn butter. One of my favorite ways is to prepare them Portuguese-style, as in the recipe below.

Preparation time: about 1 1/4 hours

1. Preheat the oven to 300 degrees.

3/4 pound linguica or
   chourico sausage

2. Stab the sausage in several places with the tines of a fork. Place it on a pie plate or small baking dish, and bake in the oven for 30 minutes to allow it to release much of its fat. Discard the fat, and set the sausage aside to cool.

3. In a 6- to 8-quart kettle, heat the olive oil over moderate heat. Add the garlic, onion and pepper, lower the heat slightly and sauté the vegetables until they are wilted, about 5 minutes.

4. When the sausage is cool enough to handle, cut it in ¼-inch-thick slices.

5. Add the sausage slices, tomatoes and white wine to the kettle. Stir to mix. Bring to a boil, lower the heat and simmer, uncovered, for 10 minutes.

6. Add the mussels, toss to coat them with the vegetables, cover them, and steam them over moderate heat for 6 to 8 minutes, or until the shells have opened. (Discard any that haven't.)

7. Divide the mussels between four large soup bowls, spooning the vegetables, sausage and broth over them. Sprinkle each portion with 1 tablespoon minced parsley. Serve immediately, accompanied by hot French bread.

Serves 4

¼ cup olive oil
4 teaspoons minced garlic
1½ cups coarsely chopped onion
1 green pepper, cored, seeded and coarsely chopped

2 large tomatoes, peeled, seeded and coarsely chopped
2 cups dry white wine

4 pounds mussels, well scrubbed, "beards" pulled off

4 tablespoons minced parsley
French bread, heated

CRISPLY SAUTÉED BAY SCALLOPS

The small, white, cylinder-shaped delicacies known as bay scallops are found in greatest profusion in the bays of Nantucket, Martha's Vineyard and Cape Cod. The only portion of the bay scallop (or of the larger sea scallop) obtainable commercially is the adductor muscle, which secures the mollusk's two shells together. (This muscle permits the scallop to open and close its shells at will, thus generating propulsion through the water.) The rest of the scallop (unlike the body of a clam, which is eaten in its entirety) is discarded—except in France, where its pink roe is considered a great prize. Some stalwart New Englanders, however, are so devoted to the bay scallop that they go out in season and gather their own—no mean feat—steam them like clams in the shell and eat the whole inside, dunked in butter. If you gather your own whole scallops, follow the recipe for Steamed Clams (p. 86). Otherwise, this is my favorite way of preparing their wonderful little muscles:

Preparation time: 30 minutes soaking; about 10 minutes cooking

3/4 *pound bay scallops*
Milk

2 *tablespoons unsalted butter*
2 *tablespoons vegetable oil*

1/2 *cup flour*
1/2 *teaspoon salt*
Freshly ground black pepper to taste
2 *eggs, well beaten*
2 *cups soft bread crumbs, preferably homemade*

1/4 *cup minced parsley (optional)*
2 *lemon wedges*

1. Place the scallops in a shallow bowl and soak them, covered in milk, at least 30 minutes or until you are ready to fry them.

2. In a 12- to 14-inch skillet, preferably one with high sides, melt the butter in the oil over moderate heat. (If scallops are confined too closely together in a small skillet, they will not crisp properly. Therefore it is very important to use what may appear to be too large a pan. If you don't have a really large one, fry them in two batches.)

3. While the butter melts, combine the flour, salt and pepper in a pie plate or on paper towelling, and, with your fingers, mix them well. Pour the eggs into a shallow bowl. Spread the bread crumbs in a pie plate or shallow bowl.

4. When the butter has melted, increase the heat to high. Working quickly, drain the scallops in a strainer. In batches, roll them in the seasoned flour, coat them with the beaten egg, and cover them on all sides with bread crumbs. Immediately drop them into the skillet, taking care not to get splattered by the hot fat and to keep the scallops separated from one another. Holding the heat high, frequently shake the pan vigorously to turn the scallops as they cook. Sauté them only until the crumbs are golden brown, about 3 to 5 minutes. Scallops cook quickly and will toughen with overcooking.

5. With a slotted spoon, remove the scallops from the skillet and divide them between two heated dinner plates. Sprinkle them with parsley, if desired, and serve them immediately, accompanied by lemon wedges.

Serves 2

BAKED SEA SCALLOPS *BOURGUIGNONNES*

Formerly frowned upon and deemed unworthy of comparison to the bay scallop, its small cousin, the sea scallop, is becoming increasingly popular. And rightly so. If correctly cooked—that is, not overcooked—sea scallops are almost as tender and delicate in flavor. Harvested by dredging in the deep Atlantic, off the New England coast, they occur in greatest profusion in Maine's icy waters.

Preparation time: about 25 minutes

1. Preheat the oven to 450 degrees. Generously butter six scallop shells or 5-inch ramekins.
2. In a mixing bowl, combine the bread crumbs, parsley, garlic, salt and pepper. Toss to mix well. Drizzle the olive oil over the crumbs, and stir until all the crumbs are moistened.

2 cups soft bread crumbs, preferably homemade
1/2 cup minced parsley
2 teaspoons minced garlic
1/2 teaspoon salt
Freshly ground black pepper to taste
1/4 cup olive oil

3. Rinse the scallops in cold water, and pat them dry with paper towelling. Divide them between the six shells or ramekins. Carefully spoon the herbed bread crumbs over the scallops, distributing the crumbs as evenly as possible and covering the scallops completely.

2 pounds sea scallops

4. Bake the scallops for 10 minutes, after which time the crumbs should be nicely toasted and brown. If not, run the scallops briefly under a broiler until the crumbs color. Take care not to cook them too long or they will toughen.
5. Dribble 1 tablespoon melted butter over each dish of scallops. Serve immediately.

6 tablespoons unsalted butter, melted

Serves 6

Cod, Haddock and Scrod

Patriot Samuel Adams said it most succinctly. "The codfish," he once wrote, "was to us what wool was to England or tobacco to Virginia: the great staple which became the basis of power and wealth."

Early New Englanders could not have survived without the cod—not just because of its nutritive value, but for economic reasons. Even before the Pilgrims' landing at Plymouth, European fishermen had made dried and salt cod the region's first export for cash. (Cod takes to salting more successfully than any other fish, and salt cod can last for years without spoiling.)

Both cod and haddock remain abundant in New England waters despite hundreds of years of fishing. Cod, a deepwater fish, is caught along the entire New England coast; the smaller haddock stays north of Cape Cod. The two fish have similar firm, white flesh. The main difference, from the cook's point of view, is the coloration of the dark skin usually left clinging firmly to the meat of the haddock.

In New England, and only there, visitors will also encounter a third, apocryphal "species:" Boston scrod. There are many possible explanations (none of them substantiated) about the derivation and meaning of the word. Some people believe "scrod" to be a contraction of "Sacred Cod," the name of the 4-foot pine sculpture that has hung in Massachusetts' State House since 1748. Food authority Waverley Root playfully defined scrod as "a young cod when it isn't a young haddock," but today the term usually refers to all young cod or haddock, about 1 to 2 pounds, that are scooped up in fishermen's nets along with larger fish. At the Parker House in Boston, "scrod" has traditionally meant the top of the catch, and therefore the freshest fish, be it cod, haddock, pollock or hake. In restaurants or fish markets, the word is often spelled "schrod." Conventional wisdom has it that the addition of the "h" means the fish is haddock; if there's no "h," it's assumed to be cod. Whatever their biological classification, cod, scrod and haddock may be used interchangeably in most recipes. What's more, the fish are unusually versatile, lending themselves to simple broiling or baking as well as more flavorful preparations.

SIMPLE BROILED SCROD

Preparation time: about 20 minutes

1. Preheat the broiler.
2. With a pastry brush, lightly coat the bottom of a shallow baking dish, large enough to hold the fillets in 1 layer, with some of the melted butter. Brush the fish fillets on both sides with the remaining butter. Arrange them in the pan, and place it under the broiler, about 5 inches from the heat.
3. Without turning the fish, broil it 5 to 10 minutes, depending on its thickness, or until the fish is opaque and firm to the touch.
4. While the fish is broiling, toast the bread crumbs. In a small skillet, melt the butter. Add the bread crumbs with the parsley, and sauté them until they are barely brown, stirring frequently. When the fish appears to be done, pat the crumbs evenly over its surface. Return the fish to the broiler for 3 to 5 minutes, until the crumbs are golden brown.

5. Serve the fillets on heated plates, garnished with sprigs of parsley and lemon wedges.

Serves 4

3 tablespoons unsalted
  butter, melted
2 pounds scrod fillets (or
  haddock or cod)

1 tablespoon unsalted butter
1/2 cup bread crumbs,
  preferably homemade
3 tablespoons minced parsley
Salt and freshly ground black
  pepper to taste

Sprigs of parsley
4 lemon wedges

POACHED CODFISH STEAKS WITH EGG SAUCE

Preparation time: about 15 minutes

1. Fill a 14-inch enameled or stainless-steel skillet to 1 inch of the top with water, and add the salt. Bring the water to a boil, reduce the heat and add the cod steaks. Simmer the steaks for about 8 minutes, or until the flesh flakes easily when pierced with the tip of a knife. Remove the steaks with a slotted spatula, and drain them on a dish towel. Arrange them on a heated platter, and serve them with Egg Sauce (recipe follows).

Serves 4

1 tablespoon salt
4 (3/4-inch) cod steaks

EGG SAUCE

1/2 cup unsalted butter
1/4 cup hot fish stock (from
  poached cod)
2 hard-boiled eggs, finely
  chopped
1 large tomato, peeled,
  seeded and finely chopped
1 tablespoon minced parsley
2 tablespoons snipped chives
Salt and freshly ground black
  pepper to taste

1. Melt the butter in an enameled or stainless-steel saucepan. With a wooden spoon, stir in the stock, eggs, tomato, parsley and chives. Add salt and pepper. Heat the sauce to the boiling point, and transfer it to a sauceboat.

Makes about 1 cup

HADDOCK AND VEGETABLES *EN PAPILLOTE*

Preparation time: about 1 hour

2 pounds haddock (or cod or
  scrod) fillets
1/2 pound thinly sliced
  mushrooms
2 cups (about 1/2 pound)
  broccoli flowerettes
1/2 pound zucchini or yellow
  squash (or both), cut in
  1/2-inch slices
1/2 pound carrots, peeled and
  cut in 1/4-inch slices
4 tablespoons unsalted
  butter
Salt and freshly ground black
  pepper to taste

1. Preheat the oven to 450 degrees. Generously butter four (18-inch) lengths of heavy-duty aluminum foil.
2. Cut the fish fillets into 1/2-pound pieces, and place one in the center of each buttered length of foil. Arrange one quarter of the mushrooms, broccoli, squash and carrots over and around each fillet. Dot each portion with 1 tablespoon butter cut into small pieces, and sprinkle with a little salt and pepper. Fold the foil up and around the fish. Seal the foil together lengthwise; then fold the ends of the package over the top and seal.

3. Bake the packages for 40 to 45 minutes, or until the fish flakes easily and the vegetables are just tender. (Test by opening just one package.) Carefully remove the fish and vegetables from the foil packages, watching for escaping steam, and transfer them to preheated dinner plates. Serve immediately, garnished with lemon wedges.

Serves 4

4 *lemon wedges*

PAN-FRIED CODFISH CHEEKS

The thought of eating fish cheeks might strike many people as downright peculiar, but in New England and eastern Canada codfish cheeks (and even tongues) are considered a great delicacy. Pan-fried, they retain a delightful, somewhat gelatinous, moist interior enhanced by a crisp, golden crust. They are not always easy to find, but persevere. They are worth the search.

Preparation time: about 15 minutes

1. In a large, heavy skillet, melt the butter with the oil over moderate heat.

2 *tablespoons unsalted butter*
2 *tablespoons oil*

2. While the butter is melting, put the flour, salt and pepper in a brown paper bag, close it tightly and shake to mix well. Open the bag, drop in half the codfish cheeks, seal tightly and shake to coat the cheeks with the flour.

½ *cup flour*
½ *teaspoon salt*
Freshly ground black pepper to taste
1 *pound codfish cheeks*

3. Remove the cheeks from the bag, dusting off any excess flour. Repeat with the remaining cheeks. Increase the heat to moderately high and place the cheeks in the butter, taking care not to get splattered by the hot fat. Fry the cheeks, turning them occasionally, for 8 to 10 minutes, until they are nicely browned on all sides. Try not to crowd them in the skillet. If the pan is not large enough, fry them in two batches, keeping the first batch warm in a preheated oven while you fry the second.

4. Transfer the cheeks to a heated platter. Sprinkle with parsley, cilantro or dill, and garnish with lemon wedges. Serve at once.

3 *tablespoons minced fresh parsley, cilantro or dill*
4 *lemon wedges*

Serves 4

FINNAN HADDIE

The name *finnan haddie* may or may not be derived, according to food authority Waverley Root, from "Findon haddock," after the town in Scotland where smoked haddock was supposedly born as a delicacy when a warehouse full of salted fish caught fire—and its flavor improved. In New England today, finnan haddie usually consists of smoked cod or haddock fillets served in a cream sauce enriched with egg yolks. Since smoked haddock can be hard to come by even in New England, finnan haddie appears on few restaurant menus. But it's served regularly on the brunch buffets at the Parker House and Ritz-Carlton hotels in Boston.

One word of warning: Smoked haddock varies in the degree of saltiness. To reduce the salt content, you may wish to soak the fish in cold water, as you would salt cod (see page 97), for an hour or more before starting to cook.

Preparation time: about 30 minutes

1 small onion, sliced and
    separated into rings
2 pounds smoked cod or
    haddock fillets
Freshly ground black pepper

1. Place the onion rings in the bottom of a deep, heavy skillet. Place the fish fillets on top, and grind fresh black pepper over them. Cover them with water. Bring the water to a boil; then reduce the heat to medium-low and poach the fish, covered, for 10 to 15 minutes, or until it flakes easily. Drain the fish, discard the onions and separate the fillets into 1- to 2-inch pieces.

2 tablespoons unsalted
    butter
2 tablespoons flour
2 cups milk
1/2 cup heavy cream
2 tablespoons strained fresh
    lemon juice
1 teaspoon Dijon mustard
1 teaspoon dry mustard
3 egg yolks, beaten

2. While the fish is poaching, make the sauce. In a medium saucepan, over moderately low heat, melt the butter. Whisk in the flour, and beat until the mixture has formed a smooth roux and is beginning to turn light brown. Slowly whisk in the milk, beating well so that no lumps form. Increase the heat to moderate, and cook the sauce about 3 minutes, or until it has started to thicken. Stir in the cream, lemon juice and Dijon and dry mustards. Remove the sauce from the heat, and allow it to cool slightly. Whisk in the egg yolks, and blend well.

3. Add the flaked fish to the sauce, and mix well. If necessary, reheat the mixture over low heat. Taste the fish and sauce for seasoning, and add salt and pepper if necessary. Serve over toast points or hot rice.

Salt and freshly ground black pepper to taste
Toast points or 3 cups cooked rice, heated

Serves 6 to 8

CAPE COD BOILED DINNER

Preparation time: 12 hours soaking; about 1 1/2 hours preparation and cooking

1. Place the salt cod in a glass or enamel bowl. Cover it with cold water, and soak it, refrigerated, for at least 12 hours, changing the water several times.

2 pounds boneless salt cod

2. Cut the tops off the beets, leaving about 1 inch of stem. Place them in a large saucepan, and cover them with water by about 2 inches. Over high heat, bring the beets to a boil. Reduce the heat to low and simmer, covered, until the beets are tender when pierced with the tip of a knife, about 30 to 45 minutes. Remove the beets with a slotted spoon, and, when they are cool enough to handle, cut off the remaining stems and slip off their skins. Return them to the hot water to keep warm while you prepare the other ingredients.

6 medium beets (about 1 1/2 pounds), well scrubbed

3. Drain the cod, and rinse it again in cold water. Place it in a saucepan, and cover it with water by 1 inch. Bring the water to a boil. Reduce the heat to low and simmer, partially covered, for 20 minutes, or until the fish flakes easily. Remove the fish from the pot with a slotted spoon and drain it on paper towelling. Allow it to cool.

4. Meanwhile, bring another large pot of water to a boil. Drop in the potatoes and let them simmer, uncovered, for 15 minutes. Add the carrots and turnips, and let the vegetables continue to simmer, uncovered, for about 10 minutes, or until they are just tender when pierced with the tip of a knife. (If they are ready before the fish, hold them in the hot water with the heat turned off.)

2 pounds new potatoes, scrubbed
1 pound baby carrots, peeled
1 pound turnips, rutabagas or parsnips, peeled and thickly sliced

*¹/₄ pound salt pork, rind
removed, cut in ¹/₄-inch
cubes*

*2 tablespoons unsalted
butter*
2 tablespoons flour
1 cup milk
1 teaspoon dry mustard
*Salt and freshly ground black
pepper to taste*

5. In a skillet, fry the salt pork, tossing it frequently, until it is crisp and golden on all sides. With a slotted spoon, remove the pieces from the pan and drain them on paper towelling. Reserve the rendered fat in the skillet.

6. Add the butter to the rendered pork fat. When it has melted, mix in the flour, stirring so that no lumps form. Slowly add the milk, mustard, salt and pepper, stirring continuously until the mixture has thickened. Simmer about 3 minutes.

7. When the fish is cool enough to handle, cut it into large chunks, discarding any remaining skin and bones. Add the fish to the white sauce, and heat it through.

8. Mound the fish in the center of a heated serving platter. Sprinkle the cooked salt pork on top, and arrange the beets, potatoes, carrots and turnips decoratively around it.

Serves 6 to 8

MARY SPILHAUS'S WHISKERY CODFISH BALLS

One of the passions of Harry Hornblower's life—besides Plimoth Plantation, which he founded—was what he called "whiskery" codfish balls. Every time he encountered codfish balls or cakes on a restaurant's menu, he would optimistically order them, hoping for the best. More often than not, he would receive flat, smooth cakes and be vastly disappointed. One weekend, visiting his cousin Mary Spilhaus in Bourne, on Cape Cod, he discovered that every Sunday she served the codfish balls of his dreams. Thereafter he contrived to have many a Sunday breakfast at Mary's. Her recipe, which follows, is all the more valuable because it does not call for mashed potatoes but utilizes dehydrated potatoes instead, a real time and labor saver.

*Preparation time: 12 hours soaking; about 45 minutes preparation
and cooking*

1. Place the salt cod in a glass or enamel bowl. Cover it with water, and soak it at least 12 hours, refrigerated, changing the water several times.

1 pound boneless salt cod

2. Pour the vegetable oil into a deep fryer or deep, heavy pot, and heat it to a temperature of 375 degrees. Preheat the oven to 200 degrees.

Vegetable oil

3. Shred the cod in a food processor fitted with a steel blade by pulsating the machine off and on several times (or shred it by hand). Reserve the cod.

4. Place the Potato Buds in a mixing bowl and, with an electric beater or a wooden spoon, beat in 2 cups boiling water. Mix well. Scrape in the shredded fish, and beat until the ingredients are thoroughly blended. Add as much of the remaining ⅔ cup boiling water as needed to have the mixture adhere to itself. (How much water you'll need depends largely on how thoroughly you drained the salt cod.) Beat in the egg.

1 (5-ounce) box Potato Buds
2 to 2⅔ cups boiling water
1 egg, well beaten

5. Drop the codfish mixture by the heaping tablespoon into the hot fat. Do not fry more than 5 balls at one time. Fry them for about 4 minutes, turning them once, or until they are golden brown on all sides. With a slotted spoon, remove the balls from the fat, and transfer them to a baking sheet lined with paper towelling. Hold them in the preheated oven until all the codfish balls have been fried.

Serves 6

GRILLED SWORDFISH WITH THYME

Swordfish is one of New England's most popular fish. While it is found all along the Atlantic coast from Newfoundland to Cuba, most swordfish caught in New England in the summer comes from Nantucket Sound, that narrow body of water bordered by Martha's Vineyard, Nantucket and Cape Cod. Swordfish meat has a firm, dense texture rather like beefsteak, and, like beefsteak, it is particularly good grilled over charcoal.

Preparation time: 30 to 45 minutes for the coals; about 15 minutes preparation and cooking

2 tablespoons unsalted
  butter, melted
1 tablespoon fresh thyme
  leaves or 1 teaspoon dried
2 tablespoons strained fresh
  lime or lemon juice
1 (1-pound) swordfish
  steak, about 1-inch thick,
  at room temperature

Freshly ground black pepper
Lime or lemon wedges

1. Prepare the charcoal fire for grilling. The coals should be red-hot but not flaming.

2. In a small bowl, combine the butter, thyme and lime juice. Stir to mix them well. With a pastry brush, generously coat one side of the swordfish with the herbed butter.

3. Place the steak, buttered side down, on the grill about 4 inches above the coals. (If your grill has a cover, use it, leaving the vents open. If not, watch carefully for flames and sprinkle any flare-up with water.) Grill the fish for 4 minutes. Brush the top side with herbed butter, and turn the fish. Grill it 3 minutes longer. Test the swordfish for doneness by pressing the flesh with a fork. It should yield slightly, but should not be mushy; mushiness indicates it hasn't cooked enough. The cooking time will vary depending on the intensity of the heat and the thickness of the steak. Take special care not to overcook the fish, or it will dry out.

4. Transfer the swordfish to a heated platter, and drizzle it with any remaining herbed butter. Grind some pepper over the top, and serve with lime or lemon wedges.

Serves 2

GRILLED OR BROILED SEAFOOD KEBABS

Swordfish has long been a popular New England fish, but fresh tuna is a relative latecomer to the scene. When it first arrived in the 1960s, it was consumed largely raw, in the guise of Japanese *sushi* and *sashimi*. Now New Englanders and our many summertime visitors are finding this hearty red-meated fish—somewhat reminiscent of beef in color—a wonderful food for grilling. The danger, as with swordfish, is overcooking, for its flesh dries out easily. Fast-cooking kebabs are an easy, surefire solution that ensures moist and tender fish.

Preparation time: 1 hour marinating; 30 to 45 minutes for the coals; about 15 minutes preparation and cooking

1. Melt the butter over low heat in a small skillet. When it liquifies, add the bay leaves and garlic. Without increasing the heat, cook the herbed butter 3 or 4 minutes, or until the bay leaves have softened slightly. Remove the pan from the heat, add the lime juice and mix well.

1/2 cup unsalted butter
10 bay leaves
3 cloves garlic, peeled and very thinly sliced
1/4 cup strained fresh lime juice

2. Pour the butter mixture into a glass or porcelain baking dish or bowl. Add the cubes of tuna and swordfish and the shrimp. Spoon the butter mixture over them until all the pieces are well coated. Cover the dish with plastic wrap, and reserve it in a cool corner of the kitchen. Allow the fish to marinate for 1 hour, turning the pieces occasionally to redistribute the marinade.

1 to 1 1/4 pounds tuna fish, cut in 1-inch cubes
1 to 1 1/4 pounds swordfish, skin discarded, cut in 1-inch cubes
12 jumbo shrimp, shelled and deveined

3. About halfway through the marinating period, preheat the broiler, or start a charcoal fire. The coals should be red-hot but not flaming.

4. Divide the fish, shrimp and tomatoes among 6 skewers, and thread them, alternating them attractively. Brush the kebabs with some of the remaining marinade. (Discard the pieces of bay leaf and garlic.)

18 cherry tomatoes

5. If you are broiling the kebabs, set them on a rack about 4 inches below the broiler element, and broil them under high heat for 2 minutes. Turn them, brush them with more marinade and broil them 2 minutes longer.

6. If you are grilling the kebabs, set them on a rack about 4 inches above the coals. Brush them with marinade, cover them with the grill lid (or a tent of aluminum foil) and grill them for 3 minutes. Turn the kebabs, brush them with more marinade, and grill them another 3 minutes.

7. Serve the kebabs immediately, garnished with sprigs of cilantro and wedges of lemon.

Sprigs of cilantro
6 lemon wedges

Serves 6

PORTUGUESE-STYLE TUNA

Provincetown, at the very tip of Cape Cod, is one of New England's most renowned tourist attractions. Many artists and writers live there, attracted both by one another's presence and the town's free-spirited bohemian life-style. During the summer, hordes of tourists descend—some coming from Boston on excursion boats, others in a steady stream of cars from different towns on the "lower Cape"—all to see the picturesque town, to visit its shops and art galleries, to eat at its many justifiably famous restaurants, to sun on its wide beaches with their encroaching sand dunes and to contemplate its picture-postcard harbor.

It is the harbor that epitomizes the spirit of the real Provincetown. Filled with all manner of vessels from simple sailboats to pristine yachts to weatherbeaten fishing craft, it is above all a working port whose fishing trawlers venture out year-round in all weather seeking the fish of the Northeast—cod, haddock, tuna, halibut, sword, mako shark, to name the most popular. As in the other major fishing ports of New England—New Bedford, Boston and Gloucester—many of the trawlers are manned by folk of Portuguese extraction whose contribution to the foodways of New England are as important as the foodstuffs they provide. The recipe that follows was adapted from a dish served in a small Portuguese restaurant in Provincetown many, many years ago, long before tuna was popular. The restaurant has long since disappeared, but its aromatic, lusty tuna dish lingers on.

Preparation time: about 1 hour

1 cup coarsely chopped
   onion
2 teaspoons minced garlic
¼ cup olive oil
⅓ pound linguica sausage,
   thinly sliced

1. In a large skillet over low heat, sauté the onion and garlic in the olive oil until they are soft, about 5 minutes. Add the sausage slices and, stirring frequently, sauté another 5 minutes.

2. Add the tomatoes, wine, oregano, salt and pepper. Mix well, and bring the sauce to a boil over moderately high heat.

2 pounds tomatoes, peeled, seeded and coarsely chopped
1½ cups dry white wine
1 teaspoon oregano
¼ teaspoon salt
Freshly ground black pepper to taste

3. Coarsely chop the kale, and add it to the tomatoes. Lower the heat, cover the pan, and simmer 2 or 3 minutes, or until the kale starts to wilt. Stir the mixture well and simmer, partially covered, 15 minutes.

½ pound kale, trimmed of tough stems and thoroughly cleaned

4. Preheat the oven to 375 degrees.
5. Transfer half the sauce to a 8-by-11-inch baking pan, or its equivalent.
6. Cut the tuna steaks into 6 more or less equal portions (tuna steaks vary in size). Arrange them on top of the tomato-kale sauce, and cover them with the remaining sauce. Place the pan in the oven, and bake 30 minutes, or until the sauce is bubbling hot. Garnish with minced cilantro or parsley.

2½ to 3 pounds tuna steaks
3 tablespoons minced cilantro or parsley

Serves 6

Bluefish

Bluefish are found the world over, yet in New England we tend to think of them as exclusively ours. Although some are as long as 4 feet, most of the local catch fall into the "snapper" or juvenile category—averaging about 18 inches. They are voracious creatures, swimming in schools, and often attacking and killing many more smaller fish than they can eat. If you go out to sea looking for them, telltale signs (besides circling gulls) are smooth slicks of water—presumably from the oil in their bodies—and an elusive odor similar to cucumber for which I've never received a plausible explanation.

As a food, bluefish has a mixed reputation. Many people do not enjoy it simply because it is oily and, like mackerel, it has to be outstandingly fresh to be good. Cooked over charcoal within hours of being caught, it is, I think, one of New England's best. If you can't catch a bluefish yourself, or if you don't have a fisherman friend who will give you one of his surplus (for when they're running in the middle of the summer, they're truly abundant), buy at a seaside fishmarket. The two recipes that follow are simple, and are guaranteed to enhance a strong-flavored fish.

CHARCOAL-GRILLED BLUEFISH

Preparation time: 30 to 45 minutes for the coals; about 10 minutes preparation and cooking

2 pounds bluefish fillets
Juice of 1 lime

1. Place the fillets skin side down on a platter. Generously squeeze the juice of a lime over the fillets, and let them rest while you prepare the charcoal.

2. Prepare the charcoal for grilling. When the coals are ready, they should be red-hot but not flaming. Oil the grill rack so the fish will not stick to it.

3. Place the fillets on the rack, skin side down, about 4 inches above the coals. (If your grill has a cover, use it. If not, watch carefully for flames and sprinkle any flare-up with water.) Cook the fish 5 minutes. With a large spatula, turn the fillets over, and cook it, uncovered, 5 minutes.

4. Test the fish for doneness. It should flake easily when pierced with the tip of a knife. If not, cook it an additional 3 to 5 minutes.

Lime wedges

5. Serve the fillets immediately, accompanied by wedges of lime.

Serves 4

BAKED MUSTARD-COATED BLUEFISH

Preparation time: about 30 minutes

1. Preheat the oven to 450 degrees.

2. In a small bowl or cup, combine the mustard and the mayonnaise, and stir well. Spread the mixture over the top of the fillets. Pat the cracker crumbs on top of the fillets.

1 tablespoon Dijon mustard
1 tablespoon unsweetened mayonnaise
2 pounds skinless bluefish fillets
10 Ritz crackers, crushed with a rolling pin

3. Place the butter in a baking dish large enough to contain the fillets in one layer. Set the dish in the oven until the butter melts. Add the fish, and bake it for 15 to 20 minutes, or until the crumbs are nicely toasted and the fish flakes easily when pierced with the tip of a knife. As the fish cooks, baste occasionally with the melted butter. Serve the fish garnished with lemon wedges and parsley.

3 tablespoons unsalted butter
4 lemon wedges
Parsley sprigs

Serves 4

SALMON BAKED IN GRAPEFRUIT JUICE

The Atlantic salmon, perhaps the most ancient of gourmet fish, spawned for centuries almost exclusively in New England's largest rivers—from the Connecticut north to Canada's St John. By the early 1800s, however, pollution and the proliferation of dams had decimated the salmon population. Today, fortunately, concerted efforts to cleanse the rivers are proving successful, and salmon are returning in increasing numbers, although not in the abundance we once knew. Happily, however, farm-raised salmon is becoming widely available, so the beautifully colored and delicate-tasting fish is once again easily obtainable.

Preparation time: about 30 minutes

1 leek (about ¹/₂ pound),
trimmed of roots and
green leaves

1 tablespoon unsalted butter
2 small salmon fillets (about
· 1 pound total), skinned
¹/₄ pound mushrooms,
trimmed of ends and
thinly sliced
¹/₂ cup strained fresh
grapefruit juice
¹/₄ cup dry white wine
¹/₄ teaspoon salt

2 tablespoons unsalted
butter, cut in two pieces

1. Preheat the oven to 400 degrees.

2. With a sharp knife, starting from ¹/₂ inch above the root end, cut the leek lengthwise down the middle. (Do not cut all the way through to the root end.) Rinse the leek under cold water, spreading the leaves apart to dislodge any grit. Shake well to remove excess water. Cut the leek crosswise into thin slices.

3. In a flameproof baking or gratin dish that is large enough to contain the salmon fillets in one layer, melt the butter over low heat. Add the leek and mushrooms, and sauté them, stirring occasionally, until they are wilted, about 5 minutes. Pour the grapefruit juice, wine and salt over the vegetables, and simmer 5 minutes longer. Remove the pan from the heat.

4. Place the salmon fillets in the baking dish, and spoon some of the vegetables and liquid over them. Set the dish on a rack near the top of the oven, and bake the fish for 10 to 15 minutes, or until it flakes easily when pierced with the tip of a knife.

5. Transfer the fillets to two preheated dinner plates, cover them loosely with foil and keep them warm.

6. Place the baking dish over high heat and, stirring constantly, reduce the liquid in it by about one-quarter. Add one piece of butter, and stir until it has melted. Repeat with the remaining piece. Spoon the sauce (it will have thickened somewhat) and vegetables over the fillets, and serve immediately.

Serves 2

STRIPED BASS STEAKS BROILED WITH DILL

The number of striped bass, once one of the most abundant fish in our waters, is—of this writing—so seriously depleted that most New England states have strict regulations on the daily number, the length and the weight of the fish allowed, to be taken. The delicately flavored white flesh of striped bass used to lend itself wonderfully to stuffing and slow oven baking, but today only the very large fish are available, generally cut into steaks.

Preparation time: 30 minutes marinating; about 25 minutes preparation and cooking

1. Preheat the broiler.
2. In a shallow baking dish large enough to contain the steaks in one layer, combine the oil, lemon juice and rind, shallots and dill. Whisk until the marinade is well blended. Add the fish steaks, turning them over to coat both sides, and marinate them for 30 minutes, turning them once or twice to recoat their surfaces.
3. Just before broiling, turn the steaks once more. Place the baking dish about 4 inches from the flame, and broil the steaks 5 to 7 minutes on each side, or until they are golden brown and the flesh feels firm to the touch.

4. Arrange the steaks on heated dinner plates, garnished with lemon wedges and accompanied by Cucumber-Dill Sauce, if desired.

Serves 4

4 (1-inch-thick) striped bass
  steaks
¼ cup vegetable oil
3 tablespoons strained fresh
  lemon juice
1 teaspoon grated lemon
  rind
1 tablespoon minced shallots
3 tablespoons finely chopped
  dill

4 lemon wedges
Cucumber-Dill Sauce
  (optional; recipe follows)

CUCUMBER-DILL SAUCE

Preparation time: about 70 minutes

1. Peel the cucumber, and cut it in half lengthwise. With a teaspoon, scrape out the seeds. Cut the cucumber crosswise in thin slices. Place them in a colander, sprinkle them with salt and leave them to drain in the sink for 1 hour.
2. In a medium-size mixing bowl, combine the sour cream and yogurt. Blend thoroughly. Add the onion, dill and pepper, and stir to mix.
3. Transfer the cucumber slices to paper towelling. Gently squeeze to draw off any residual moisture. Add the cucumber to the yogurt mixture, and toss to mix the sauce.
4. Serve at room temperature.

Makes about 2 cups

1 cucumber
½ teaspoon salt

¾ cup sour cream
1 cup unflavored yogurt
3 tablespoons grated onion
½ cup minced fresh dill
¼ teaspoon freshly ground
  black pepper

MICROWAVE-POACHED HALIBUT
WITH CILANTRO BEURRE BLANC

Atlantic halibut, a large flat fish, cousin to the flounder, lives in the cold waters off New England's coast at a depth of two hundred to three thousand feet. Its flesh is pristine white and firm, and it has a delicate flavor that marries well with buttery sauces such as hollandaise or beurre blanc.

Preparation time: about 30 minutes

1 tablespoon finely chopped
shallots
1/2 cup dry white wine
1 tablespoon strained fresh
lemon juice
12 tablespoons unsalted
butter, at room
temperature

1. Place the shallots in a small nonreactive saucepan, and cover them with the wine and lemon juice. Bring the liquid to a boil over high heat, and boil it, uncovered, until almost all of it has evaporated, leaving only 1 tablespoon remaining in the pan. Reduce the heat to low, and remove the pan from the heat.

2. Stir in 1 tablespoon butter and, with a whisk, beat it until it has been completely incorporated. Return the pan to the heat, and repeat with the remaining 11 tablespoons of butter, 1 tablespoon at a time. Do not allow the pan to become so hot that the butter melts and separates. Remove the pan from the heat if it threatens to do so.

Freshly ground white pepper
to taste
Salt to taste
3 tablespoons minced fresh
cilantro (or fresh
tarragon)

3. Add pepper and salt. (If you want, strain the sauce at this point.) Stir in the cilantro. Keep the sauce warm in a bath of warm, not hot, water while you microwave-poach the fish. Stir the sauce occasionally.

2 pounds halibut fillets, cut
into four equal portions
1/2 cup dry white wine

4. Position the halibut pieces in a microwave-safe baking dish large enough to contain them in one layer. Pour the wine over the fish. Cover the baking dish tightly with plastic wrap, and cook the fish in the microwave oven at full strength for 5 to 10 minutes, depending on the oven's wattage and the thickness of the fish. Turn the pan a quarter round halfway through the cooking.

5. Serve the fish on heated dinner plates, and ladle a generous spoonful of the cilantro beurre blanc over it.

Serves 4

Spring comes slowly to New England. Snow clings tenaciously to northern slopes. The earth looks gray and sodden. Only the willows, with their hint of green, hold promise. When spring does arrive, though, it comes first to the rivers. Suddenly, sometime between late March and mid-April, when the lowland shadbush is a bouquet of white blossoms, there is a burst of activity in our streams as herring (or alewives, as we New Englanders call them) and shad return to start their journey upstream to spawn. Inside both female varieties is a culinary treasure: roe, or sacs of tender eggs. The shad's roe are larger, a pair often weighing a pound, while the herring's roe may be as little as two or three ounces. I love them both, but, because the herring's are so small and delicate, I guess I love them just a little bit more.

Preparation time: 1 hour soaking; about 10 minutes cooking

1. Carefully cut the sacs of roe apart, trying not to tear the delicate membrane. Place them in a shallow dish, and cover them with milk. Soak them for at least 1 hour.

1 pound fresh herring roe, rinsed
1/2 to 1 cup milk

2. Place the roe on paper towelling, and pat them as thoroughly dry as possible.

3. In a pie plate or on another piece of towelling, combine the flour, salt and pepper, and mix them well. In a small skillet, melt the butter over moderate heat until it turns a light brown. Remove it from the heat, and reserve it.

1 cup flour
1/2 teaspoon salt
Freshly ground black pepper to taste
4 tablespoons unsalted butter

4. Melt 2 tablespoons butter in a skillet large enough to hold all the roe in one layer without too much crowding. (Use the remaining 2 tablespoons butter if you need to cook the roe in two batches.) Gently roll the roe sacs in the flour mixture, shaking off any excess. When the butter is foaming, add the roe. Fry them approximately 1 to 1 1/2 minutes on each side, over moderately high heat, until they are golden brown.

2 to 4 tablespoons unsalted butter

1 tablespoon minced parsley
2 lemon wedges

5. Arrange the roe on heated plates, and dribble the brown butter over them. Sprinkle them with parsley, and garnish them with the lemon wedges.

Serves 2

NEW ENGLAND FISH STEW

It must be admitted that this recipe is not a New England tradition, being more of a cioppino than anything else. But it deserves to be included in this book, since it uses New England seafood exclusively and always receives rave reviews.

Preparation time: about 1 1/4 hours

½ cup olive oil
2 teaspoons minced garlic
1 large onion (about ¾ pound), coarsely chopped

4 cloves
2 teaspoons fennel seed
4 teaspoons grated orange rind
2 large tomatoes (about 1 pound), peeled and chopped

1. Preheat the oven to 350 degrees.
2. In a 10- to 12-quart flameproof casserole, heat the oil over moderate heat. Add the garlic and the onion. Stirring frequently, cook until they are wilted, about 10 minutes. Remove the casserole from the stove.

3. Add the cloves, fennel, orange rind and tomatoes to the casserole, and mix well.

4. Layer the fish, scallops, clams, mussels, shrimp and lobster pieces—in that order—on top of the tomato mixture.

5. Place the casserole in the middle of the oven, and bake 45 to 60 minutes, stirring the shellfish two or three times during the baking for more even cooking. Bake until the mussel and clam shells are wide open. (After 1 hour, discard any that have not opened.)

2 pounds fish fillets (your choice of one or more: cod, scrod, haddock, bass, bluefish, salmon, swordfish), skinned and cut in chunks
1 pound sea scallops
30 littleneck clams (about 4 pounds), scrubbed
30 mussels (about 2 pounds), scrubbed, "beards" pulled off
1/2 pound unpeeled shrimp
2 (1 1/2-pound) lobsters, uncooked, bodies and claws cut into 2-inch segments (let your fishmonger do this for you)

6. Just before serving, sprinkle with cilantro or parsley.

7. Serve the stew in large soup bowls, with an even mix of ingredients. Ladle generous helpings of the broth over the seafood. The stew should be served with warm, crisp French bread to soak up the juices.

1/2 cup minced fresh cilantro or parsley

Serves 8

VIII

Meats, Poultry and Game

ROAST TURKEY WITH CHESTNUT AND SAUSAGE STUFFING

Most Americans consider the harvest feast held in Plymouth in the fall of 1621 as the very first Thanksgiving, the inspiration for the holiday as we celebrate it today. Yet what we call Thanksgiving is really a blend of three earlier traditions: the joyous English custom of celebrating a successful harvest, called Harvest Home; the solemn, prayerful religious event of thanks-giving itself that was held—almost spontaneously—at any time of the year in gratitude for any number of fortuitous blessings; and the commemoration of the Pilgrims' landing, known as Forefathers' Day (December 21).

In fact, very little is known about the 1621 event in Plymouth; only two references give us some insight about the food available and the celebration itself. One is from Edward Winslow:

Our harvest being gotten in, our governor sent four men on fowling, that we might after a special manner rejoice together after we had gathered the fruit of our labors. They four in one day killed as much fowl as, with a little help beside, served the company almost a week. . . . At which time, many of the Indians coming amongst us . . . whom for three days we entertained and feasted, and they went out and killed five deer. . . .

And the second from William Bradford's *Of Plimmoth Plantation:*

All the summer there was no want; and now began to come in store of fowl, as winter approached, of which this place did about when they came first . . . and besides waterfowl there was a great store of wild turkeys, of which they took many, besides venison, etc. . . .

Preparation time: about 5 to 6 hours, depending on the size of the turkey

STUFFING

1. Preheat the oven to 275 degrees.
2. Place the bread cubes on a cookie sheet or jelly roll pan, and toast them in the oven, stirring them occasionally, until they are dry and barely brown.

1 (1-pound) loaf white bread, trimmed of crusts and cut into 1/2-inch cubes

3. Transfer the bread cubes to a large mixing bowl, and sprinkle them with the salt, thyme, pepper and oregano. Toss the cubes to mix them well with the seasonings. Increase the oven heat to 400 degrees.

2 teaspoons salt
1 teaspoon thyme
1 teaspoon freshly ground black pepper
1 teaspoon oregano

4. In a large frying pan, melt the butter over moderately low heat. Add the onion, and sauté it, stirring occasionally, until it is soft, about 10 minutes. Add the crumbled sausage meat, and simmer, stirring, for 5 minutes. Add the celery, and cook another 5 minutes. Remove the pan from the heat, and add the parsley. Toss the ingredients to mix them.

1 cup unsalted butter
2 cups finely chopped onion
1 pound sausage meat, crumbled
1 cup finely chopped celery
1/2 cup minced parsley

5. With a sharp knife, cut an X on the round side of each chestnut. Place the chestnuts on a baking sheet, and roast them for 20 minutes, or until their shells have cracked. While the chestnuts are still hot, peel off both layers of skin with a knife (hold the chestnuts in a potholder while doing so). Coarsely chop them. With a rubber spatula, scrape the onion-sausage mixture on top of the bread. Add the eggs and chestnuts, and, with two large spoons, mix the stuffing thoroughly. Set it aside.

1 pound chestnuts
3 eggs, beaten

ROAST TURKEY

1 (18- to 20-pound) turkey
Salt
Freshly ground black pepper

½ cup unsalted butter,
   melted

1. Preheat the oven to 425 degrees.

2. Remove the neck and giblets from the turkey, and reserve them for making stock. Rinse the turkey inside and out, pack the cavities with paper towels and dry it completely. Season the cavities and skin of the turkey with salt and pepper, and loosely stuff the body and neck cavities with the chestnut stuffing. Sew up the openings, truss the bird, if desired, and place it, breast side up, in a large roasting pan. Roast it for 30 minutes.

3. Reduce the heat to 350 degrees. Place a double thickness of cheesecloth over the turkey's breast, and generously brush it with a portion of the melted butter. Roast the turkey, basting it with the remaining melted butter and the pan juices, every 20 to 30 minutes for 3 hours or longer, or until the juices run clear when the thigh is pricked with the tines of a fork. (While the turkey is roasting, make the stock; recipe follows.) Transfer the turkey to a heated platter, and remove the cheesecloth and trussing strings. Allow the turkey to rest 20 minutes or so before carving it. (Meanwhile, make the gravy; recipe follows.)

Serves 12 to 16

TURKEY STOCK

Turkey neck
Turkey giblets (gizzard,
   heart and liver)
1 carrot, broken in 3 pieces
1 stalk celery, broken in 3
   pieces
1 small onion, quartered
6 sprigs parsley
1 teaspoon salt
6 cups chicken stock or
   water

1. Place the turkey neck, gizzard and heart in a 3- to 4-quart saucepan along with the carrot, celery, onion, parsley and salt. Pour the stock into the pan, and stir to mix the ingredients. Bring the stock to a boil, reduce the heat to low and simmer, covered, for 2 hours. Add the liver, and simmer 15 minutes longer.

2. Remove the stock from the heat, and strain it through a fine sieve. Reserve it for the gravy. Discard the vegetables, but save the heart, gizzard and liver. Chop them for use in the gravy.

Makes about 4 cups

1. From the roasting pan drippings, skim off all but ½ cup turkey fat. Over moderate heat, sprinkle the flour over the pan, and, with a wooden spoon, scrape up all the particles clinging to the bottom. Stir until the flour is well blended with the fat.

2. Add the turkey stock, stirring constantly to prevent lumps from forming. Lower the heat, and cook 10 minutes. Strain the gravy into a saucepan, and stir in the chopped giblets. Transfer the gravy to a heated gravy boat, and serve it with the turkey.

Pan drippings
½ cup flour

4 cups hot turkey stock
Salt and freshly ground black pepper to taste
Chopped cooked giblets

Makes about 4 cups

NEW ENGLAND CHICKEN POT PIE

New England Chicken Pot Pie is different from most other chicken pies in that its crust is not the traditional pastry topping. Instead, the pie is covered with baking powder biscuits, whose bready consistency has a nice way of absorbing the good sauce beneath. In New England, chicken pot pie is traditionally served Christmas morning, something that has always struck me as singularly puzzling. I mean, why would you want to eat it for breakfast when, presumably, you would be following it with a turkey dinner? I personally forego this particular tradition, but eat the pie with relish any time the rest of the year.

Preparation time: about 5 hours

1. Fill a kettle (large enough to contain the chicken compactly) half full with water. Stir in the salt. Stud the onion pieces with the cloves. Add the chicken, onion, bay leaves, carrot and celery to the pot. (If the water does not cover the chicken completely, add sufficient to do so.) Bring the water to a boil, lower the heat and simmer the chicken, partially covered, for 1¼ to 1½ hours, or until it is tender when pierced in the thigh with a fork. (Turn the chicken over once during the cooking period.) Remove the chicken from the pot, and set it aside to cool.

1 (6-pound) roasting chicken
1 tablespoon salt
1 medium onion, halved
4 cloves
2 bay leaves
1 carrot, broken in 3 pieces
2 stalks celery, broken in 3 pieces

2. When the chicken is cool enough to handle, remove and discard its skin. Tear the meat off the bones, cutting it into generous chunks, about 1 to 2 inches each. Reserve the meat. Return the bones to the cooking broth, set the kettle back on the heat and simmer the liquid, uncovered, until it has reduced by half, about 1½ hours.

3. Strain the chicken stock into a bowl. Cool it. Place the stock in the refrigerator or freezer, and leave it there until the fat, which will have risen to the surface, has solidified.

1 pound mushrooms, halved or quartered, according to size
2 (10-ounce) packages frozen pearl onions, thawed
1 tablespoon unsalted butter
1 red pepper, cored and seeded, cut in ½-inch dice

4. Meanwhile, place the mushrooms in a steamer, and steam them until they are barely tender, about 4 minutes. Set them aside with the onions. Melt the butter in a small skillet over moderate heat, and sauté the pepper until it is barely tender, about 5 minutes. Reserve it.

4 tablespoons chicken fat
4 tablespoons flour
2 teaspoons salt
Freshly ground black pepper to taste
3 cups chicken stock
1 cup light cream
2 teaspoons tarragon

5. When the chicken fat has solidified, scrape off 4 tablespoons and drop it into a 2-quart saucepan. Melt the fat over low heat. Add the flour and, stirring constantly, blend it well with the fat. Mix in the salt and pepper. Slowly add the chicken stock, stirring constantly, so that as it cooks and thickens no lumps form. Stir in the cream. Add the tarragon. Cook, stirring, until the sauce just comes to a boil and has thickened. Remove it from the heat.

6. In a large casserole, combine the chicken with the reserved mushrooms, onions and peppers. Pour the sauce over the mixture, and toss to mix thoroughly. (The pie may be prepared in advance to this point, then refrigerated and held for the final baking. Be sure to remove it from the refrigerator at least 1 hour before baking to bring the ingredients to room temperature.)

7. Preheat the oven to 450 degrees.

8. In the bowl of a food processor fitted with a steel blade, place the flour, salt and baking powder. Whirl until they are well combined. Drop the pieces of butter and lard through the feed tube. Whirl until the mixture resembles coarse meal. Add the tarragon. Pour in the cream, and whirl until the dough just begins to adhere to itself. (Or mix the dough by hand or in an electric mixer.)

9. Turn the dough out on a lightly floured surface, knead it briefly and, with a rolling pin, roll it into a circle about $^1/_3$-inch thick. With a cookie cutter, cut it into 2-inch rounds. Reroll the scraps, and cut additional rounds. Cover the top of the pie with the rounds, setting them together as closely as possible without overlapping.

10. Place the pie in the oven, and bake for 25 minutes, or until the crust is golden brown.

Serves 8

2 to 2$^1/_4$ cups flour
$^1/_2$ teaspoon salt
1 tablespoon baking powder
2 tablespoons unsalted
    butter, well chilled and
    cut in pieces
2 tablespoons lard, well
    chilled and cut in pieces
1$^1/_2$ teaspoons tarragon
$^1/_2$ cup light cream

NEW ENGLAND BOILED DINNER

New England Boiled Dinner seems to be part and parcel of the New England heritage. For those who lived inland in the early days, away from the sea and the easy availability of fresh fish, meat like lamb and beef was the ready alternative. Old-time recipes suggest that perhaps these meats were not as tender as we know them today, for most were either stewed, boiled, pot-roasted or chopped. Further, there was always the problem of preservation, so many meats were smoked, salted or "corned."

New England Boiled Dinner was the Northeast's version of corned beef and cabbage, but with the addition of a lot of vegetables. I am including the traditional ones here, but no one will fault you for choosing your own favorites—perhaps turnips, rutabagas, parsnips or shell beans. The trick lies in the timing—having everything cooked, tender and steaming hot at the same moment.

You may question the abundance of the dinner. The practical New England housewife had a trick up her sleeve: by producing more than was humanly possible to consume at the first meal, she had lots of leftovers for the second, if not the third.

Preparation time: about 4 hours

1 (4- to 5-pound) corned beef brisket

1. Wash the brisket in cold water. Place it in a large, 6- to 8-quart kettle, and cover it by 1 inch with water. Bring the water to a boil, skim off any of the scum that accumulates, lower the heat and simmer, covered, for 3 to 4 hours, or until the meat feels tender when pierced with a knife. (Check the pot occasionally, refilling it if the water gets too low.)

(About 45 minutes before the meat is finished, start preparing and cooking the vegetables. They can be cooked with the beef, but most people prefer to cook them separately, particularly the beets. Allow 30 to 45 minutes for the beets, 20 to 30 minutes for the potatoes, 15 to 20 minutes for the carrots, 10 to 15 minutes for the onions and cabbage. If your vegetables take longer than you anticipate, do not worry. The beef can hold without spoiling in its own hot broth.)

2 bunches small beets, trimmed and scrubbed

2. Place the beets in a saucepan, cover them with water and bring the water to a boil. Lower the heat and simmer the beets, partially covered, for about 30 minutes, or until they offer no resistance when pierced with the tip of a knife. (Allow more time if the beets are large.) With a slotted spoon, remove them from their water, and slip off their skins.

1½ pounds red potatoes, scrubbed

3. Place the potatoes in a saucepan, cover them with water and bring the water to a boil. Lower the heat, and simmer the potatoes for 20 to 30 minutes, depending on their size, or until they are tender. Drain them.

1 pound carrots, peeled and cut in 2-inch pieces

4. Place the carrots in a saucepan, cover them with water and bring the water to a boil. Lower the heat, and simmer the carrots for 15 to 20 minutes, or until they are tender. Drain them.

¾ pound white onions, peeled
2 pounds cabbage, cut in sixths and cored

5. Fill a large saucepan two-thirds full with water, and bring the water to a boil. Add the onions and cabbage, and simmer them until they are tender, about 15 minutes. Drain them.

6. Serve the boiled dinner by placing the corned beef in the center of a large heated platter and surrounding it with the vegetables. Garnish with parsley. Serve the dinner accompanied by horseradish and mustard.

Parsley sprigs
Horseradish
Dijon mustard

Serves 8 to 10

RED FLANNEL HASH

Red Flannel Hash basically uses the leftovers from a New England Boiled Dinner (see p. 117). One non–New Englander, visiting my family one year and taken with the name, was clearly disappointed after his first bite. "Why, it's nothing but corned beef hash with beets!" he exclaimed. But most New Englanders think it's pretty tasty. When they make the Boiled Dinner, they always make sure they're generous with the ingredients so there's enough left over for the hash. The important thing, according to strict traditionalists, is that the meat and vegetables be chopped, not ground in a meat grinder. They claim that "newfangled" grinders reduce the ingredients to a mash—and they're right.

Preparation time: about 1¼ hours

1. Preheat the oven to 350 degrees.
2. In a 12-inch cast-iron skillet (one that can be put in an oven), fry the salt pork over moderate heat until it is crisp and brown and has rendered all its fat. With a slotted spoon, remove the pieces to paper towelling to drain. Pour all but 3 tablespoons of the fat into a cup, and reserve it. Add the onion to the skillet and, over low heat, sauté it until it is wilted, about 5 minutes.

¼ pound lean salt pork,
* rind removed, cut into*
* ¼-inch cubes*
½ cup finely chopped onion

3 cups coarsely chopped
  boiled potatoes
2 cups finely chopped boiled
  corned beef
1½ cups chopped cooked
  beets
1 teaspoon Worcestershire
  sauce
¼ to ⅓ cup light cream
Salt and freshly ground black
  pepper to taste

3. In a large mixing bowl, combine the cooked onions, potatoes, corned beef, beets, reserved salt pork cubes, and ¼ cup cream. Toss the ingredients to mix them, adding more cream if necessary to bind them. Add salt and pepper to taste.

4. Pour the reserved fat into the original skillet, tipping the skillet and swirling the fat around so the bottom of the skillet is well coated. Add the hash, spreading it evenly. Set the skillet in the oven, and bake the hash 35 to 45 minutes, or until the top is nicely browned.

Serves 6

BEEFSTEAK PUDDING WITH DILL

It wasn't until 1624 that the first cattle were imported into Plymouth, and for some years there were so few of them they were too valuable to be consumed. When one Pilgrim died in 1633, his cow and calf were appraised at £20—exactly twice the value of his house and garden. As the cattle population increased, its worth diminished, and, by the second half of the century, beef, pigs, goats and sheep—as well as venison, fish and wildfowl—were part of the diet.

The following recipe was inspired by one from an old English cookbook, for a beef pie that incorporated a bottom and top crust of Yorkshire pudding, not pastry. The pie didn't quite work out for me as described in the recipe, but the combination of tastes was too good to be dismissed, so I offer my alternative: separate cooking of the stew and pudding, and combining them only as they go to the table—thus achieving puffy, crisp bottom and top.

Preparation time: about 3 hours

1. Place the oil and butter in a large frying pan, preferably one with high sides, over moderately high heat. While they are heating, combine the flour, salt and pepper in a paper bag, close the bag tightly and shake well to mix. Add half the cubes of beef, close the bag again and shake vigorously to coat the meat with flour. Shake off any excess flour.

2. When the oil is hot and the butter foaming, add the floured meat and sauté it, turning it frequently, until it is brown on all sides. With a slotted spoon, transfer it to a flame-proof casserole. Flour and sauté the remaining meat.

3. Rinse out the frying pan with water.

4. Return the frying pan to moderately low heat, and melt the butter. Add the garlic and onions, and, stirring frequently, sauté them until they are just wilted, about 5 minutes. Toss in the mushrooms, and sauté them 3 to 4 minutes, or until they are barely softened.

5. With a rubber spatula, scrape the vegetables into the casserole.

2 tablespoons vegetable oil
1 tablespoon unsalted butter
½ cup flour
½ teaspoon salt
Freshly ground black pepper to taste
2 pounds top-round steak, trimmed of fat and cut in ¾-inch cubes

2 tablespoons unsalted butter
1 teaspoon minced garlic
¾ cup coarsely chopped onions
⅓ pound mushrooms, trimmed of ends and quartered or halved, depending on size

6. Add the carrots, beef stock, Worcestershire sauce, salt and dill. Mix well. (If there isn't sufficient stock to cover the other ingredients, add stock or water to barely cover them.) Bring the liquid to a boil, reduce the heat and simmer the stew, covered, for 1½ hours, or until the meat is tender. Stir the stew occasionally during the cooking period.

7. Preheat the oven to 450 degrees.

2 large carrots, peeled and coarsely chopped (about 1 cup)
2 cups beef stock, preferably homemade
1 tablespoon Worcestershire sauce
½ teaspoon salt
3 tablespoons minced fresh dill

8. Place the cornstarch in a cup or small bowl. With a spoon, transfer approximately ½ cup gravy from the stew to the cup or bowl, and mix it with the cornstarch until no lumps remain. Pour the mixture back into the stew, and stir until the gravy thickens. Keep the stew on the lowest possible setting while you make the Yorkshire pudding.

9. In a small frying pan, over very low heat, render the suet.

2 tablespoons cornstarch

⅓ pound beef suet, cut into ½-inch-thick slices

4 tablespoons rendered suet

10. Into a 9-by-12-inch baking pan, or its equivalent, pour 4 tablespoons of the melted suet. Tip the pan so that its bottom and sides are well coated with the fat. Set the pan in the oven to heat.

2 eggs
1/2 cup milk
2 tablespoons rendered suet
1 cup flour
1/4 teaspoon salt
1/4 cup minced fresh dill

11. In the jar of an electric blender, combine the eggs, milk, suet, flour, salt and dill, and whirl until they are well blended. Pour the mixture into the heated baking pan, and bake 15 minutes. Reduce the heat to 350 degrees, and bake an additional 15 minutes.

12. Remove the pan from the oven, and cut the Yorkshire pudding into 3-inch squares. Place a square on a heated dinner plate. Spoon a portion of stew on top, then cover with a second piece of pudding. Serve immediately.

Serves 6

FRIZZLED BEEF

Before refrigeration and freezing, cooks had to devise other methods of providing a steady food supply without spoilage. Frizzled beef, essentially dried thinly sliced beef, is a legacy from the Indians, who dried much of their game.

Preparation time: about 30 minutes

1/2 pound dried beef, thinly
  sliced
1 quart water

1. Taste the dried beef to determine the degree of saltiness. To remove excess salt, bring the water to a boil and parboil the beef slices for about 10 seconds. Drain them. When the slices are cool enough to handle, tear them into 1-inch pieces, and reserve the pieces. (If the meat is not too salty, do not blanch it; simply tear it into pieces.)

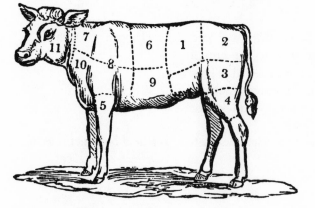

2. In a 2- to 3-quart saucepan, melt the butter. Sauté the shallots and mushrooms over moderate heat, stirring occasionally. When the mushrooms have exuded their juices, add the dried beef. Stir well to coat the meat with the pan juices. Continue to cook, stirring, over moderate heat, until the meat has begun to crinkle (or "frizzle"). Take care not to brown the meat.

2 tablespoons unsalted butter
2 tablespoons finely chopped shallot
1/2 pound mushrooms, thinly sliced

3. In a small saucepan, melt the butter. Add the flour and, with a wooden spoon, stir until it has absorbed the butter. Cook it for 1 minute to eliminate any raw taste. Mix in the mustard. Slowly add the cream, stirring constantly so that no lumps form. Continue cooking, stirring occasionally, until the mixture has thickened. Add the sherry, mix to blend the sauce, and simmer it until it is thoroughly heated.

1 tablespoon unsalted butter
1 tablespoon flour
1/2 teaspoon dry mustard
1 cup light cream
1/4 cup dry sherry

4. With a rubber spatula, scrape the cream sauce into the saucepan containing the beef and mushrooms. Mix well. Add salt and pepper.

Salt and freshly ground pepper to taste

5. Arrange two pieces of toast or one English muffin, toasted and split, on each warm dinner plate. Spoon the Frizzled Beef over them, and serve immediately.

4 to 6 slices bread, toasted, or 2 to 3 English muffins, split and toasted

Serves 2 to 3

POACHED LEG OF LAMB WITH HORSERADISH SAUCE

Beacon Hill, in the center of Boston, is one of the loveliest residential areas in the entire United States—or so I think. Often dating from the early eighteenth century, handsome private homes—some converted into apartments—line the streets of the steep hill, and gas lamps illuminating the brick sidewalks flicker 24 hours a day. This unusual English recipe for poached leg of lamb was given to me by a most charming lady who, although she lives in solitary splendor in a classic brick house midway up the hill, loves to entertain. She often serves it in the heart of winter, when the snows swirl across the city, obscuring the tall, modern buildings of Boston's financial district, and Beacon Hill seems part of an age gone by.

Preparation time: about 1³/4 hours

1 (7- to 8-pound) leg of
  lamb, bone in
2 cloves garlic, peeled and
  cut in slivers

2 teaspoons salt
3 stalks celery
2 bay leaves
3 cloves garlic, peeled and
  cut in half lengthwise
2 sprigs fresh rosemary
10 peppercorns
5 cloves

8 leeks, trimmed of roots
  and green leaves

1 pound carrots, peeled and
  cut in 1-inch lengths
8 small red potatoes (about
  2 pounds), scrubbed
1 small savoy cabbage, cut
  in eighths and cored

1 recipe Horseradish Sauce
  (recipe follows)

1. Cut away all the lamb's fat and fell, the membrane encasing it. Weigh it. For pink lamb, calculate the cooking time at 10 minutes per pound. With the tip of a sharp knife, make small incisions at even intervals all over the leg. Insert a sliver of garlic in each hole.

2. Place the lamb in a 24-inch fish poacher or in a kettle large enough to contain it and all the vegetables that will accompany it. Cover the lamb with cold water. Add the salt, and stir to mix. Distribute the celery, bay leaves, garlic, rosemary, peppercorns and cloves evenly around the leg. Set the poacher over two burners, and partially cover it. Bring the water to a boil over high heat; this will take about 20 to 30 minutes. Skim off and discard all foam that rises to the surface.

3. With a sharp knife, starting from ½ inch above the root end, cut each leek lengthwise down the middle. (Do not cut all the way through to the root end.) Rinse the leeks under cold water, spreading the leaves apart to dislodge any grit.

4. To facilitate later removal of the vegetables from the cooking broth, wrap the leeks, then the carrots, in double-thick lengths of cheesecloth, and securely tie both packages. Wrap the potatoes together in the same manner, but wrap each wedge of cabbage individually.

5. After the water has come to a boil, calculate the time remaining for the lamb to cook (it should be between 40 to 50 minutes). When there are 30 minutes left for the lamb to cook, add the packages of leeks, carrots and potatoes to the water.

6. When there are 15 minutes left, add the cabbage packages.

7. When the lamb has finished cooking, remove it from the poaching liquid. (The liquid may be saved for use in a soup or discarded.) Allow the lamb to rest 5 minutes, then slice it. Unwrap the vegetables. Arrange the lamb slices decoratively on a heated serving platter, and place the vegetables around it. Serve the poached lamb accompanied by Horseradish Sauce (recipe follows).

Serves 8

HORSERADISH SAUCE

1. In a bowl, combine the sour cream, mustard and horseradish, and blend them well. (If you like your sauce sharper, add more horseradish.) Transfer the sauce to a sauceboat.

Makes about 2 cups

2 cups sour cream
1 tablespoon Dijon mustard
About 2 tablespoons horseradish

FRUITED LAMB STEW

While lamb is not a particularly popular meat in the United States, it has always ranked high with the folk of New England, who raised it from the very beginning on their small farms. This stew, featuring two of our major crops, apples and cranberries, is a true New England dish. (By the end of the cooking time, the fruit will have disappeared, but not its flavors!) If you have the time to make the stew a day or two ahead, do so. Its flavors develop nicely with age.

Preparation time: about 2¹/₂ hours

1. Pour the oil into a 14-inch skillet, preferably one with high sides. Set the skillet over high heat to bring the oil almost to the smoking point.

2. While the oil heats, put the flour, salt and pepper into a paper bag. Close the bag securely, and shake the contents vigorously to mix them well. Add a generous handful of the lamb cubes. Seal the bag again, and shake well to coat the lamb with the seasoned flour. Carefully drop the pieces into the hot oil, and sauté them over high heat, turning them frequently, until they are browned on all sides. (Do not crowd them in the skillet; the lamb will not brown properly if you do.) As they are done, transfer the lamb with a slotted spoon to a bowl. Repeat until all the pieces are browned, adding more oil if necessary.

3. Rinse the skillet clean.

¹/₃ cup vegetable oil

³/₄ cup flour
1 teaspoon salt
¹/₂ teaspoon freshly ground black pepper
3 pounds boneless stewing lamb, trimmed of all fat and cut in 1¹/₂-inch cubes

2 tablespoons vegetable oil
2 tablespoons unsalted
  butter
2 cups coarsely chopped
  onion
2 teaspoons minced garlic
1½ cups cranberries,
  washed and picked over
2 large apples, cored, peeled
  and thinly sliced

4. Place the skillet over moderately low heat. Add the vegetable oil and butter, and, when the butter is melted, add the onion and garlic. Sauté them until they are soft, about 5 minutes. Add the cranberries and apples, and cook them, stirring occasionally, until the apples have softened, about 10 minutes.

1½ teaspoons thyme
4 cups chicken stock,
  preferably homemade

5. With a rubber spatula, scrape the contents of the skillet into a 4- to 6-quart casserole. Add the reserved browned lamb and thyme. Toss the ingredients to mix them. Pour in the chicken stock. Bring the liquid to a boil, lower the heat and cover the casserole. Simmer the stew, stirring occasionally, for 1½ hours.

2 large russet potatoes
  (about ⅔ pound each),
  peeled and cut crosswise
  into ¼-inch slices
1 pound carrots, peeled, cut
  in thirds crosswise, then
  cut lengthwise into
  "sticks"
1½ pounds small white
  onions, peeled

6. Add the potatoes, carrots and onions to the stew. Mix well to distribute the vegetables evenly. Continue simmering the stew, covered, over low heat until the vegetables are tender, about 30 to 40 minutes.

3 tablespoons minced parsley

7. Sprinkle the parsley over the stew and serve it, steaming, direct from the casserole.

Serves 8

ORANGE-MARINATED ROAST LOIN OF PORK

Although the Pilgrims were not the first to bring the pig to North America—Hernando de Soto landed thirteen near Tampa in 1542—they introduced them into the colony within a few years of their arrival. Pigs soon proliferated in New England, so that by 1640 Massachusetts was carrying on a lucrative trade in salt pork, the principal form in which the animal was consumed. While salt pork figures in a number of our recipes—most notably chowder and baked beans—we are not limiting our book to that use of pork alone. This recipe for a boneless, marinated loin would surely have pleased some of the early settlers, who were not averse to an occasional roast of pork themselves.

Preparation time: 6 to 12 hours marinating, about 1 hour preparation and roasting

1. In a nonreactive roasting pan large enough to contain the loin of pork, combine the garlic, orange rind, cumin, orange juice, marmalade, oil and soy sauce. Stir briskly until the marmalade is dissolved and the ingredients are well combined. Add the loin of pork, turn it two or three times to coat it well with the marinade, and let it rest in the marinade, refrigerated, for at least 6 but not more than 24 hours. Turn the pork occasionally to redistribute the marinade. Remove the meat from the refrigerator at least 1 hour before roasting to bring it to room temperature.

2. Preheat the oven to 450 degrees.

1 3-pound boneless loin of pork
2 teaspoons minced garlic
2 tablespoons grated orange rind
2 tablespoons toasted cumin seed
1/2 cup strained fresh orange juice
2 tablespoons orange marmalade
1/4 cup vegetable oil
2 tablespoons soy sauce

3. Remove the pork from the marinade, and wipe it dry with paper towelling. Grind a generous amount of pepper over the surface of the pork. With a rubber spatula, scrape the marinade into a small saucepan. Add the white wine, and stir to mix.

4. Place the pork in a clean roasting pan, and roast it for 40 minutes.

5. While the pork is cooking, set the saucepan of marinade over a high flame, and reduce it by one-third. Hold it over low heat until the pork is done.

6. Carve the pork in 1/3-inch-thick slices, and serve it accompanied by the marinade sauce.

Freshly ground black pepper
1 cup dry white wine

Serves 6

PORK PIE

The concept of the pie—that is, a filling packed between two crusts—came to the Northeast from the Old World. It was a popular method of rendering fruit or meat more palatable and of using up leftovers. As dwellings became more sophisticated, ovens in New England were specifically constructed to contain pies (a 10-pie oven, a 20-pie oven). Nor were the hardy housewives slow to turn the harshness of the winter to their advantage: they baked pies in large quantities, and stored them in their houses in unheated "cold closets," where the pies would promptly freeze, in snowbanks, or, if worse came to worst, dangled from the branches of trees. New England winter pies were perhaps the first use of freezing as a deliberate method of food preservation.

Preparation time: about 1 hour

2 tablespoons unsalted
    butter
2 teaspoons minced garlic
1 red pepper, cored, seeded
    and cut in ¹/₂-inch dice

1. Preheat the oven to 375 degrees.
2. Melt the butter in a skillet. Add the garlic and pepper and, over moderate heat, cook them until the pepper just begins to wilt, 3 or 4 minutes. Remove the skillet from the heat, and set it aside.

2 tablespoons cornstarch
1 cup chicken stock,
    preferably homemade
¹/₂ teaspoon salt
Freshly ground black pepper
    to taste

3. In a cup, combine the cornstarch with the stock and, with the back of a spoon, mix until the cornstarch is dissolved and there are no lumps. Pour the mixture into the skillet, and return the skillet to moderate heat. Cook the gravy, stirring, until it thickens. Add the salt and pepper. Stir to blend them in.

3 cups cooked pork (or other
    leftover meat), cut into
    bite-size pieces
1 cup frozen peas, thawed
1 recipe Flaky Pie Pastry for
    a 2-crust pie (see p. 183)

4. In a bowl, combine the pork, peas and pepper mixture and, with two spoons, toss until they are well mixed. Scrape the contents into the prepared pie shell, moisten the edges of the pastry, and secure the covering crust on top, crimping the two together. With a sharp knife, cut a few slashes in the top crust so that steam can escape during the baking.
5. Bake the pie for 40 minutes, or until it is golden brown.
6. Serve the pie immediately, cut in wedges (if you don't plan to freeze it).

Serves 6

MUSTARD-CRUSTED ROAST LEG OF VENISON

As do many areas of the country, New England has its fair share of enthusiastic hunters who, like the first settlers, climb out of warm beds in the dark, cold hours before dawn to seek the wild birds and animals sharing the land. This recipe was given me by a friend who not only is an enthusiastic hunter but relishes cooking his bounty himself. Here is his recipe for a leg of venison, which, because of its ample size, he likes to serve at Christmas-party buffets.

Preparation time: about 3 hours (for a 10-pound leg)

1. Preheat the oven to 350 degrees.
2. Check the weight of the leg. Calculate the cooking time, allowing 14 minutes per pound.

1 leg of venison (about 10 pounds), trimmed of all tough skin and cut at the knee joint (reserve the shank for another use)

3. With the tip of a paring knife, make small incisions at regular intervals all over the roast. Insert a sliver of garlic in each hole. In a small bowl, combine the flour, mustard, salt and pepper, and mix them well.

2 to 3 cloves garlic, thinly sliced
1/2 cup flour
1 tablespoon dry mustard
1/2 teaspoon salt
Freshly ground black pepper to taste

4. With a pastry brush, coat the top side of the leg with melted butter. Sprinkle half the flour mixture over the buttered surface of the venison, and pat the flour so that it adheres well. Place the meat in a roasting pan, floured side up, and roast it for one-half of the total cooking time.

2 tablespoons unsalted butter, melted

*2 tablespoons unsalted
  butter, melted*

5. Turn the roast over. Brush the new top side with the melted butter, and coat it with the remaining flour mixture. Return the roast to the oven, and bake it for the remaining time, or until a meat thermometer registers 140 degrees when inserted into the center of the roast (but not touching the bone). If in doubt, make a deep cut with a carving knife near the center of the roast 5 minutes before it is due to be finished cooking. The meat should be pink, but not bloody, and very juicy. Watch the cooking time carefully. Since venison is so lean, overcooking badly toughens the meat. If it is not done to your taste, however, return the roast to the oven and cook 15 minutes longer before testing again.

*Sprigs of watercress
Red currant or Beach Plum
  Jelly (see p. 160)*

6. Remove the meat from the oven, and allow it to rest 30 minutes before serving it. Then place it on a warm platter, and garnish the meat with watercress. (The pan juices may be thickened with a small amount of flour, if desired, and served with the roast.) Serve the roast accompanied by red currant or Beach Plum Jelly.

Serves 20

SAUTÉED PHEASANT WITH CRANBERRIES AND PORT

Pheasant is probably the most popular feathered game in New England. Yet it is not native to the land, or even the country. It hails, in fact, from China. How it came to our parts remains a mystery, although there is substantial evidence that the birds were introduced here as early as the middle of the nineteenth century, and that they swiftly adapted themselves to their new habitat. Certainly one of my fondest recollections as a child was the authoritative call of one fat, beautifully marked male who favored the bayberry bushes behind our house on Cape Cod, but who would brazenly, fearlessly, stroll across our lawn every morning. Each summer, when I returned from the city, I would listen for his cry, always fearful that perhaps some hunter had killed him during the previous season. But he was too crafty, at least for seven years. Then there was silence, and my favorite pheasant was heard no more.

Preparation time: about 40 minutes

1. Cut the pheasant in half. Cut away the backbone and breast bone. Refrigerate the pheasant halves while you make the stock: Place the bones, along with the wing tips, neck, gizzard and heart in a small saucepan. Add the celery, onion and salt. Pour on the water. It should cover the bones by ½ inch; if not, add some more. Bring the liquid to a boil, reduce the heat to low and simmer, covered, for 2 hours. Strain the stock into a small bowl. Discard the bones and vegetables. There should be about ¾ cup stock. Set it aside.

1 (2- to 3-pound) pheasant, cleaned and dressed, with gizzard and heart reserved
½ stalk celery
½ small onion, peeled
Pinch salt
2 cups water

2. Combine the butter and vegetable oil over high heat in a large frying pan with 4-inch sides. When the butter is foaming, carefully lay the pheasant halves, skin side down, in the pan. Cover the pieces with a salad plate, weighted down with unopened cans of food, to hold the meat as close as possible to the bottom of the skillet so that it browns most effectively. Keeping the heat moderately high, sauté the pheasant for 8 minutes. Remove the weighted plate, turn the pheasant to its other side, weight it again, and sauté for 6 to 8 minutes on the second side. Remove the pheasant to two heated dinner plates, and cover each loosely with foil.

1 tablespoon unsalted butter
1 tablespoon vegetable oil

3. Drain off all fat remaining in the skillet. With the heat still moderately high, add the stock and reduce it by one-half, stirring constantly. Add the relish and port, stirring briskly. When the sauce thickens somewhat, quickly spoon it over the pheasant, and serve immediately.

¾ cup pheasant stock
¼ cup Raspberry-Cranberry Relish (see p. 150) or ¼ cup Pureed Cranberry Sauce (see page 149)
2 tablespoons tawny port

Serves 2

IX
Vegetables and Beans

DURGIN-PARK'S BOSTON BAKED BEANS

Boston isn't called "Beantown" for nothing. Brown Bread (see p. 50) and baked beans have been a traditional Saturday night supper for longer than anyone now living can remember. Fish balls (see p. 98) and reheated beans make a fine New England lunch, or even a Sunday breakfast for those with hearty appetites. In days gone by, homemakers would mix up their own versions of baked beans on a Saturday morning, then carry them in stoneware crocks to the neighborhood brick-oven bakery, where the beans would slow-cook all day.

Sadly, most baked beans consumed today come out of a can. Perhaps this recipe, adapted from the method used at Boston's famous Durgin-Park restaurant, the undisputed king of Boston beaneries, will inspire modern cooks to forego the can and bake beans the old-fashioned way.

Edward Hallett, Durgin-Park's "chief bean man" for many years, offers a word of warning: "You can't let the pot just set in the oven. You've got to add water as necessary to keep the beans moist. And you can't be impatient and add too much water at a time and flood the beans."

Preparation time: about 12 hours, including soaking

1. Place the beans in a 2- to 3-quart saucepan, and cover them by 3 inches with water. Over high heat, bring the water to a boil. Remove the beans from the heat, and allow them to soak overnight.

2. In the morning, drain the beans in a colander and return them to the saucepan, covering them with fresh water. Add the baking soda, mix well, and bring the water to a boil. Continue boiling for 10 minutes. (Watch the pot carefully; the baking soda will foam and can easily boil over.) Drain the beans again, rinsing them with cold water.

3. Preheat the oven to 300 degrees.

4. Place half the salt pork cubes in the bottom of a stoneware crock or large ovenproof casserole. Ladle the beans over them. Place the rest of the pork cubes on top of the beans.

5. In a small saucepan, bring the water to a boil. Add the brown sugar, molasses, salt, mustard, ginger and vinegar, and stir until all the ingredients have dissolved. Pour the mixture over the beans, and mix well.

6. Bake the beans, covered, for about 3 hours, adding more water as necessary to keep them moist. The beans are done when they are tender and brown and have taken on the flavor of the sauce. Do not bake them so long that they disintegrate.

Serves 6 to 8

1 pound pea or navy beans (small white beans), washed and picked over

1 teaspoon baking soda

½ pound salt pork, trimmed of rind and cut in ½-inch cubes

2 cups water
¼ cup dark brown sugar
¾ cup dark molasses
1 teaspoon salt
1 teaspoon dry mustard
1 teaspoon ground ginger
2 tablespoons cider vinegar

FIDDLEHEAD FERNS IN BROWN BUTTER

Every spring in New England, about the same time the herring start running, bright green ferns, shaped like the head of a fiddle, start poking their way up through the dull, dead leaves. Undoubtedly some very brave and hungry soul at some time tasted one, and, lo! a new delicacy was born. Tasting like a lovely cross between asparagus and spinach, fiddleheads make an unusual addition to a late-spring meal and, nowadays, can be found fresh in season on supermarket shelves throughout the Northeast.

Preparation time: about 15 minutes

¹/₂ teaspoon salt
¹/₂ pound fiddlehead ferns,
cleaned and trimmed

1. Fill a 2- to 3-quart saucepan with water to within 2 inches of its rim, and add the salt. Bring the water to a boil. Drop in the fiddleheads, and cook them over moderate heat until they are tender, about 5 minutes. Immediately drain them, and rinse them under cold water to stop them from further cooking. Drain them again.

4 tablespoons unsalted
butter
¹/₄ teaspoon salt
Freshly ground black pepper
to taste

2. Melt the butter in a 12-inch skillet over moderately high heat, shaking the pan vigorously until the butter just starts to turn brown and smell nutty, about 2 minutes. Be careful not to let the butter burn. Add the fiddleheads, toss to coat them all in the brown butter, and cook them until they are just reheated. Season them with salt and pepper. Serve them immediately.

Serves 4

HARVARD BEETS

Harvard Beets have been a tradition in New England for about as long as anyone can remember. How did they get the name? Everyone seems to have forgotten. Harvard College was founded in 1636, but it seems unlikely they were served that long ago. Harvard's official color, however, is crimson, and certainly the beets are that.

Preparation time: about 1¹/₄ hours

2 bunches medium beets,
trimmed and scrubbed

1. Place the beets in a large saucepan, cover them with water by 2 inches, and bring the water to a boil. Reduce the heat, and simmer them, partially covered, for 30 to 45 minutes, or until they offer no resistance when pierced with a knife. (Timing depends on the size and age of beets.) Drain the beets, reserving 1 cup of the liquid.

2. When the beets are cool enough to handle, cut off the root ends, slip off the skins, and cut the beets crosswise into ¹/₄-inch slices. Set them aside.

3. Melt the butter in a 3- to 4-quart saucepan. When it is foaming, add the cornstarch, and stir to blend it in. Slowly pour in the reserved beet juice, and cook the mixture, stirring constantly, until it is slightly thickened and smooth. Add the sugar, vinegar, salt and cloves. Mix until the sauce is well blended.

4. Add the sliced beets to the sauce, toss them to coat them, and, over moderately low heat, cook them, covered, until they are heated through, about 5 to 8 minutes.

2 tablespoons unsalted butter
1 tablespoon cornstarch
1/4 cup brown sugar
1/4 cup cider vinegar
1/2 teaspoon salt
1/4 teaspoon ground cloves

Serves 6

CORN PUDDING

To be at its best, Corn Pudding should be made with the freshest corn possible—never frozen. It is a delicate dish, full of the natural sweetness of the corn.

Preparation time: about 1 1/2 hours

1. Preheat the oven to 350 degrees. Put a kettle of water on to boil. Generously butter a shallow casserole or baking dish. (The wider the casserole, the shallower the pudding, and the more quickly it will set.)

2. In a medium-large mixing bowl, beat the eggs until they are frothy. Beat in the butter, salt, pepper and cream. Add the corn kernels and the nutmeg, and stir to mix. Pour the corn mixture into the prepared casserole.

3. Set the casserole in a baking pan, and fill the baking pan with boiling water halfway up the side of the casserole. Bake until the custard has set, about 1 to 1 1/2 hours. A knife inserted in the center of the custard should come out clean. Serve immediately.

4 eggs
4 tablespoons unsalted butter, melted
1/2 teaspoon salt
Freshly ground black pepper to taste
2 cups light cream
4 cups fresh corn kernels (cut from 4 large ears of corn)
1/4 teaspoon freshly grated nutmeg

Serves 8

SUMMER SUCCOTASH

For some New Englanders the name "succotash" means only one dish: Plymouth Succotash, served once a year in celebration of Forefathers' Day, December 21, when the Pilgrims landed in Plymouth. It is a curious combination of hulled corn (lye-soaked hominy), dried beans, winter vegetables, chicken, corned beef and salt pork—a feast perhaps only palatable to tradition-minded Plymouthians. Summer Succotash limits itself to two summer vegetables, beans and corn, and a generous bath of cream.

Preparation time: about 20 minutes

1 teaspoon salt
1 pound green beans,
  trimmed and cut into
  1-inch pieces
2 cups fresh corn kernels
  (cut from 2 large ears
  corn)

1. Fill a 3- to 4-quart saucepan with water, and add the salt. Bring it to a boil over high heat. Drop in the beans and cook them, uncovered, for 5 minutes. Add the corn kernels, and cook 1 minute longer. Immediately drain the vegetables, and rinse them under cold water.

3 tablespoons unsalted
  butter
3/4 cup heavy cream
Salt and freshly ground black
  pepper to taste

2. Melt the butter in a large skillet over moderate heat. When it starts to foam, add the corn and beans, and cook them, stirring constantly, until they are heated through, about 2 minutes. Pour in 1/4 cup of the cream, and stir over moderate heat until it has almost cooked away. Repeat with the remaining 1/2 cup cream, 1/4 cup at a time. Add salt and pepper, and serve immediately.

Serves 6

GARDEN VEGETABLE MEDLEY WITH OREGANO

It's a great convenience for the host to present a dish that's several foods in one. This potato and vegetable medley is precisely that; a combination of fresh vegetables common to New England truck gardens that cooks together in happy harmony. One of the chief reasons for its gustatory success is the dominance of fresh oregano among the vegetables. The early settlers made great use of fresh herbs, and the small gardens planted beside their houses offered easy access to a ready supply.

Preparation time: about 3 hours

1. Preheat the oven to 375 degrees. Brush the sides and bottom of a 9-by-12-inch glass baking dish with olive oil to prevent the vegetables' sticking.

2 tablespoons olive oil

2. Cut the potatoes into 1/8-inch-thick slices, and spread the slices over the bottom of the baking dish. Sprinkle them with the salt and pepper, and drizzle the olive oil over the top.

2 pounds boiling potatoes, peeled
1/2 teaspoon salt
Freshly grated black pepper to taste
2 tablespoons olive oil

3. Without peeling the eggplant, cut it into 1/2-inch-thick rounds, and cut each round into six wedges. Scatter the wedges on top of the potatoes. Sprinkle with the oregano.

1 (1-pound) eggplant, ends trimmed
2 tablespoons minced fresh oregano (or 2 teaspoons dried)

3 small zucchini (about 1/3 pound each), cut in 1/2-inch slices

1 red pepper (about 1/3 pound), cored, seeded, and cut into thin julienne strips

1 green pepper (about 1/3 pound), cored, seeded, and cut into thin julienne strips

1 medium red onion (about 1/3 pound), cut in half and thinly sliced

2 tablespoons minced fresh oregano (or 2 teaspoons dried)

3 large tomatoes (about 1 1/2 pounds)

2 tablespoons minced fresh oregano (or 2 teaspoons dried)

1/2 teaspoon salt

Freshly ground black pepper to taste

1/2 pound mushrooms, trimmed of ends and quartered

1/3 cup olive oil

2 tablespoons minced fresh parsley

4. Layer the zucchini slices, the red and green pepper strips and the onion on top of the eggplant. Sprinkle with the oregano.

5. Cut the tomatoes in half crosswise, and cut each half in six wedges. Arrange the tomatoes on top of the zucchini, sprinkle with the oregano, salt and pepper and top with the mushrooms. Finally, drizzle the olive oil over the vegetables.

6. Cover the baking dish tightly with a double thickness of aluminum foil, pressing down on the vegetables to compress them somewhat. Bake for 30 minutes, or until the natural juices of the vegetables are starting to bubble around the potatoes. Remove the aluminum foil, and continue to bake for 1 1/2 hours.

7. Sprinkle the vegetables with parsley, and serve them directly from the baking dish.

Serves 8

BAKED MUSHROOM-STUFFED SQUASH

Dairy products have always played an important role in New Englanders' economy and diet. The early settlers depended heavily on "white meats," as they called them, for sustenance in the early summers, when food preserved for the preceding winter had been depleted and the summer's bounty had not yet arrived.

Zucchini or yellow summer squash stuffed with bread crumbs, mushrooms and cheddar cheese can be either a hearty side dish or a light, meatless main course. Although any cheddar cheese will do, Vermont's famous cheddar gives the stuffing an authentic New England tang.

Preparation time: about 1 hour

1. Preheat the oven to 350 degrees.
2. Split each squash lengthwise. Using a spoon or a melon baller, scoop out the pulp, leaving a ½-inch-thick shell. Take care not to pierce the skin. Coarsely chop the pulp. Rub the insides of each half shell with ½ tablespoon butter, and set the shells aside.

4 medium zucchini or yellow summer squash (about ½ pound each), trimmed of stems
4 tablespoons unsalted butter, softened

3. In a skillet over medium heat, melt the butter. Sauté the onion until it is wilted, about 5 minutes. Add the mushrooms, red pepper and reserved squash pulp, and sauté them until they are soft, stirring frequently.

2 tablespoons unsalted butter
¼ cup finely chopped onion
¼ pound mushrooms, finely chopped
1 small red pepper, cored, seeded and finely chopped

4. Remove the saucepan from the heat. To the squash mixture add 1 cup of the cheese (reserving the rest for the topping), the bread crumbs, the parsley, the oregano and the egg. Stir until the cheese has melted and the mixture is well blended. Mix in the salt and pepper.

½ pound mild cheddar cheese, grated
½ cup soft bread crumbs, preferably homemade
1 tablespoon minced parsley
1 teaspoon oregano
1 egg, well beaten
Salt and freshly ground black pepper to taste

4 tablespoons pine nuts

5. Mound the cheese mixture in the reserved squash shells. Transfer the shells to a large, low-sided baking dish, and pour enough water into the dish to cover the bottom by about ¼ inch. Sprinkle each squash boat with ½ tablespoon pine nuts, and top each with ½ tablespoon of the reserved grated cheese. Bake the stuffed squash uncovered about 25 minutes, or until the shells are tender when pierced with the tip of a knife and the tops are starting to brown.

Serves 8 as a side dish, 4 as a main dish

MINTED ZUCCHINI WITH YOGURT

When zucchini vines start bearing, they bear with a vengeance, even in the far reaches of mountainous northern New England. Each summer the beneficiaries of nature's overabundance go begging for new ways to use their crop, from zucchini casseroles to zucchini muffins to zucchini soufflés. Here's a simple dish with the appealing flavors of yogurt and fresh mint to enhance the squash. Since zucchini cooks quickly and yogurt tends to separate if heated too long, leave this dish for preparation at the very last minute.

Preparation time: about 15 minutes

6 medium zucchini (about 3 pounds), trimmed of stems
2 tablespoons unsalted butter

1. Split the zucchini in half lengthwise, and thinly slice them. In a large skillet, melt the butter. When it is foaming, sauté the zucchini slices over medium heat, stirring constantly, until they are just tender but not soft, about 5 minutes.

³/₄ cup unflavored yogurt
¹/₂ cup minced fresh mint leaves
Salt and freshly ground black pepper to taste

2. Reduce the heat to low. Stir in the yogurt and mint leaves. Warm gently, stirring, until the yogurt has heated through. Add salt and pepper. Serve immediately.

Serves 8

SCALLOPED POTATOES AND TURNIPS

The French use the word *navet*, or turnip, to indicate an artistic flop (much as we use the word *turkey*). In olden Europe, before the introduction of America's potato, turnips were the lowly vegetable of the poor, if not fodder for the animals. Yet the turnip must have had some fans, for there is evidence that Jacques Cartier planted turnip seeds in Canada in 1540, and records indicate turnips growing in Massachusetts by 1629.

New England gardeners appreciate root vegetables such as parsnips, rutabagas and turnips. Not only do they continue growing well into the cold weather, their taste seems to improve with a touch of frost. Moreover, root vegetables have enormous staying power, remaining crisp and fresh-tasting for months as long as they're kept cool. In fact, before refrigeration, root cellars sustained New England farmers, allowing them to enjoy hearty, satisfying vegetables throughout the winter.

Preparation time: about 1 hour

1. Preheat the oven to 350 degrees. Generously butter a 2-quart casserole or baking dish.

2. Layer the potato, turnip and onion slices in the baking dish, dotting with butter and sprinkling with salt and pepper between layers.

4 medium potatoes (*about 2 pounds*), *peeled and thinly sliced*

1 turnip (*about 1 to 1 1/2 pounds*), *peeled and thinly sliced*

1 medium onion (*about 1/4 pound*), *peeled and thinly sliced*

2 tablespoons unsalted butter

1 teaspoon salt

Freshly ground black pepper to taste

About 2 cups light cream
2 tablespoons unsalted
   butter

2 tablespoons minced parsley

3. Add sufficient cream to the dish to cover the vegetables. Dot the top with butter. Bake the vegetables, uncovered, for 40 to 45 minutes, or until they are tender when pierced with the tip of a knife and the top is beginning to color.

4. Sprinkle the top of the vegetables with parsley, and serve immediately.

Serves 8

MASHED EASTHAM TURNIPS

One of the ways to distinguish a native Cape Codder from a visitor is the manner in which he pronounces the name of the town Eastham. The native comes out with a twangy "East-HAM," heavily accenting the second syllable, while the uninitiated hits the "East" and swallows the "ham." The town itself, a small one confined by the Atlantic on the east and Cape Cod Bay on the west, is famous for three unrelated reasons: It marks the beginning of the Cape Cod National Seashore Park, established in 1961, a magnificent 27 thousand acres of rolling hills, pitch pine, scrub oak, dunes, and sand, swaddled by the sea; one of its bay beaches, First Encounter Beach, is the spot where the Pilgrims made their first landing in the New World; and, last but not least, it is the home of a highly coveted, cream-colored turnip, the Eastham turnip—the same size and shape as its orange-hued cousin but with pale white flesh and an infinitely more delicate flavor.

Preparation time: about 45 minutes

1 Eastham turnip (about 3
   pounds; or 1 regular
   turnip or rutabaga),
   peeled and cut in 1/2-inch
   cubes
1 teaspoon salt

1. Place the turnip in a large saucepan, cover it with water, and add 1 teaspoon salt. Stir to dissolve the salt. Bring the water to a boil, lower the heat and simmer the turnip, partially covered, until it is very tender when pierced with the tip of a knife, about 25 to 30 minutes.

2. Drain the turnip. Either press it through a food mill, or, with electric beaters, whip it in the saucepan until it is nicely pureed.

3. Return the saucepan to low heat and, beating continuously, incorporate the butter, pepper, heavy cream and nutmeg. Beat until the mixture is smooth. Taste for seasoning, and add the remaining ¹/₂ teaspoon salt if desired.

3 tablespoons unsalted butter
Freshly ground black pepper to taste
¹/₃ cup heavy cream
¹/₂ teaspoon freshly grated nutmeg
¹/₂ teaspoon salt (optional)

Serves 6

MAPLE-BAKED TURNIPS

The turnip has a strong flavor, which tends to become even more pronounced when the vegetable has been in cold storage for the better part of a winter. One way to sweeten the pot, so to speak, is to bake thinly sliced turnip with another New England product: maple syrup.

As early as 1609, Mark Lescarbot, a contemporary of Champlain's, wrote that the Indians of northern New England "get juice from the trees and from it distill a sweet and agreeable liquid." European settlers soon acquired a taste for it as well. Today, as soon as winter wanes and the sap starts running, producers in Vermont, New Hampshire and parts of Massachusetts begin tapping their sugar maple trees. Creative cooks everywhere prize maple sugars and syrups—and not just for pancakes.

Preparation time: about 1¹/₄ hours

1. Preheat the oven to 350 degrees. Generously butter a 2-quart casserole or baking dish.

1 turnip (about 1½ to 2
  pounds), peeled and cut
  in ¼-inch slices
¾ teaspoon salt
Freshly ground black pepper
  to taste
¼ cup pure maple syrup
2 tablespoons granulated
  maple or dark brown
  sugar
2 tablespoons unsalted
  butter

2. Place the turnip slices in the baking dish, sprinkling salt and pepper between the layers. Dribble the maple syrup evenly over the slices. Sprinkle the sugar on top, and dot with the butter. Bake the turnip, covered, for 1 hour, or until it is tender when pierced with the tip of a knife. Serve immediately.

Serves 6

BAKED PARSNIPS

Parsnips used to command far more attention than they do today. Like turnips, they were one of the staple vegetables of Europe— until potatoes became popular in the nineteenth century and displaced them. The colonists first brought parsnips to South America in 1564, to Virginia in 1608 and to Massachusetts in 1629. And rumor has it that even the local New England Indians took a fancy to them.

Preparation time: about 30 minutes

1½ pounds parsnips, peeled
  and trimmed
½ teaspoon salt

2 tablespoons unsalted
  butter
1 tablespoon strained fresh
  lemon juice
½ teaspoon freshly grated
  nutmeg

1. Place the parsnips in a saucepan, cover them with cold water, and add the salt. Bring the water to a boil over high heat. Reduce the heat and simmer, partially covered, for 5 minutes, or until the parsnips are barely tender. Drain them, and let them cool.
2. Preheat the oven to 450 degrees.
3. Generously butter a 10-inch round tart pan (or its equivalent) with 1 tablespoon of the butter. Cut the parsnips lengthwise into ¼-inch-thick slices. Arrange the slices overlapping in the pan, in an attractive pattern. Dot the top with the remaining tablespoon of butter. Sprinkle with the lemon juice and nutmeg.

4. Bake the parsnips in the oven for 15 to 20 minutes, or until they are very hot and flecked with brown. Garnish them with the minced parsley, and serve immediately.

3 tablespoons minced parsley

Serves 4

CREAMED ONIONS

Most people think of onions not so much as a vegetable, but as a flavoring—something to be sliced to garnish a hamburger, tossed in a salad, or chopped to season sautéed dishes. Yet no New England Thanksgiving would be complete without a side dish of creamed onions. The smaller the onions, the better; tiny pearl onions give the dish an elegant look, although any white onion up to 1½ inches in diameter will do. As with any dish that requires quantities of onions, preparing creamed onions can be a weepy affair; parboiling them whole to loosen the skins helps.

Preparation time: about 1 hour

1. Drop the onions, unpeeled, into a saucepan of boiling water, and parboil them for about 1 minute. Drain them in a colander, and rinse them with cold water. Cut off the root ends and, squeezing from the opposite end, pop the onions out of their skins.

2 pounds small white onions

2. Return the onions to the saucepan, and cover them with water. Bring the water to a boil, reduce the heat to low and simmer the onions, covered, until they are tender but not soft (about 10 minutes for pearl onions, 15 for larger ones). Drain the onions again.

3. Melt the butter in the saucepan. Add the flour, and mix well. Stirring constantly, slowly add the cream, and cook the sauce over medium heat until the mixture begins to thicken. Return the onions to the pan, and add the salt and pepper. Stir gently to mix. Reduce the heat to low, and simmer the onions until they are thoroughly reheated. The cream sauce should just coat them. Serve the onions immediately, sprinkled with nutmeg.

4 tablespoons unsalted butter
1 tablespoon flour
1 cup light cream
Salt and freshly ground black pepper to taste
1 teaspoon freshly grated nutmeg

Serves 6 to 8

ACORN SQUASH WITH MAPLE SYRUP

Even among imaginative cooks, winter squash is often a victim of habit. New Englanders have such an abundance of squash, and in so many varieties, that they tend to fall back on standard preparations. But small varieties of squash, such as acorn, lend themselves to simple, elegant preparations in their own shells. This version uses our local maple syrup as both the flavoring and, in effect, a dipping sauce as well.

Preparation time: about 1 hour

2 acorn squash (about 1
  pound each; or 2 small
  butternut squash)
4 teaspoons unsalted butter,
  melted

1. Preheat the oven to 400 degrees.
2. Wash the squash, and cut them in half lengthwise. Scoop out and discard the seeds. With a pastry brush, coat the cut surfaces with butter.

4 tablespoons unsalted
  butter
1/2 cup pure maple syrup
Salt and freshly ground black
  pepper to taste

3. Arrange the squash halves, cut side up, in a baking dish. In each half, place 1 tablespoon butter and 2 tablespoons maple syrup. Dip the pastry brush in the maple syrup, and brush the cut surfaces. Sprinkle the squash with salt and pepper. Pour enough water into the pan around the squash to cover the bottom of the pan by about 1/2 inch.
4. Bake the squash for 30 to 45 minutes, or until it is tender when pierced with the tip of a knife.

Serves 4

CRANBERRY BEANS WITH PARSLEY AND GARLIC

Every August some New England vegetable stands feature, along with the mountains of other delectable fresh vegetables, a long, red and white mottled bean known as the cranberry bean, shell bean or Christmas bean. Few people know what to do with it; most just boil it. While there is nothing wrong with plain boiled cranberry beans, the addition of a bit of parsley and garlic vastly improves this oft-overlooked variety. The parsley, of course, also renders the dish a bit more attractive. When cooked, the poor cranberry bean loses its bright color and becomes, alas, an ordinary beige.

Preparation time: about 20 minutes

1. Place the cranberry beans in a small saucepan, add the salt and cover the beans with water by 1 inch. Bring the water to a boil, lower the heat and cook the beans, partially covered, for 10 minutes or until they are tender.

2. While the beans are cooking, melt the butter in a small skillet. Add the garlic, and sauté it over moderately low heat, stirring occasionally, until it is soft, about 5 minutes. Remove the skillet from the heat.

3. When the beans are tender, drain them in a strainer. Return them to the saucepan and, with a rubber spatula, scrape the garlic and butter over them. Toss to mix. Set the beans back on the heat for a minute or two to reheat them. Add the parsley, mix again and serve the beans immediately.

1 1/2 pounds fresh cranberry beans, shelled
1/2 teaspoon salt

2 tablespoons unsalted butter
1 teaspoon minced garlic

3 tablespoons minced parsley

Serves 4

THREE STEAMED FALL VEGETABLES

Most people regard parsnips and carrots as most pedestrian vegetables, but steamed and highlighted with bright green broccoli flowerettes, they become a truly special combination.

Preparation time: about 25 minutes

1. Place the parsnips and carrots in a steamer over briskly boiling water. Cover and steam the vegetables until they are just tender, about 12 to 15 minutes.

1 pound parsnips, peeled and cut in 1/2-inch cubes
1 pound carrots, peeled and cut in 1/2-inch cubes

2. Toss the broccoli on top of the parsnips and carrots, cover them and steam them 5 minutes, or until the broccoli is barely tender and still bright green.

1/2 pound broccoli flowerettes

2 tablespoons unsalted
   butter
$1/3$ cup light cream

3. Drain the water out of the bottom pan of the steamer. Transfer the vegetables to it. Add the butter and the cream. Set the pan over low heat and, stirring gently, mix until the butter has melted and the vegetables are lightly coated with hot cream.

4. Serve immediately.

Serves 8

X

Relishes, Conserves and Jellies

PUREED CRANBERRY SAUCE

As a symbol of Thanksgiving, cranberry sauce comes in second only to the turkey itself. The Pilgrims called the berries "craneberries," because, it is speculated, the curve of their young buds resembled the head of the English crane. The Indians ate them raw or cooked, unsweetened; combined them with venison to make a form of pemmican; and also used them as a dye. Later, seamen recognized them as natural scurvy preventives, thanks to their high vitamin C content.

One of only three native American fruits (along with the blueberry and the Concord grape) to find wide acceptance today, the cranberry grew wild in such profusion that no one thought to cultivate the vines until around 1816. Today cranberries are Massachusetts' largest crop, grown mainly in the bogs of Plymouth County, Cape Cod, Nantucket and Martha's Vineyard. At harvest time, 90 percent of the bogs are flooded and harvested "wet," after machines called water beaters agitate the berries loose from their vines. Floating to the surface, they create a vast, surreal crimson sea. Only berries harvested "dry," with the aid of mechanical pickers, find their way to the retail market as whole uncooked berries.

Tart cranberries may be used in quick breads, stuffings and desserts (see p. 180). As a sauce, they may be cooked or uncooked, served plain or flavored, smooth or chunky, jellied or liquid. Two versions follow: a cooked puree and an uncooked relish. According to taste, either one may be served with hot roast turkey, used in sandwiches the next day, or eaten by the spoonful by its most loyal adherents.

Preparation time: about ¹/₂ hour plus chilling

1 pound package
   cranberries, washed and
   picked over
1 apple, unpeeled but cored
   and sliced
³/₄ cup sugar
1 cup water

1. In a saucepan, combine the cranberries, apple, sugar and water, and mix them well. Bring them to a boil over moderately high heat, then reduce the heat to low. Simmer, covered, until all the berries have popped, about 15 minutes.
2. Transfer the mixture to a food mill, and press it through into a bowl. Discard all residue. Allow the sauce to cool to room temperature, then refrigerate it, covered with plastic, until serving time. (It should be served chilled.)

Makes about 4 cups

RASPBERRY-CRANBERRY RELISH

Some neighbors on Cape Cod, Sandy and Tom Delnickas, have a tradition of roasting turkey on the beach in celebration of Labor Day. They invite all their friends, and it's a day-long festive affair that we all look forward to each year, a happy conclusion to summer. All I can say is that turkey never tastes as good as when it's been baked over charcoal and caressed by sea breezes. Sandy serves this piquant relish with the bird, but it's also wonderful with other fowl (see Sautéed Pheasant with Cranberries and Port, p. 130).

Preparation time: about 10 minutes

12 ounces cranberries

1. In a food processor fitted with a steel blade, or by hand, coarsely chop the cranberries. Transfer them to a mixing bowl.

2. Add the diced apple, marmalade and raspberries. Pour in ³/₄ cup sugar, and mix well. Taste for sweetness, and add up to ³/₄ cup more sugar if desired.

3. Chill or serve at room temperature.

Makes about 3 cups

1 red apple, unpeeled but
   cored and diced small
¹/₂ cup tart orange
   marmalade
1 (10-ounce) package
   frozen raspberries, thawed
   and drained
³/₄ to 1¹/₂ cups sugar,
   according to taste

Preserving Relishes by Water Bath

The following boiling-water bath is suitable for canning acidic foods such as fruits and vinegared relishes. In each bath, process only one type of food, in the same size containers. Refer to individual recipes for exact processing times, if processing is required.

1. Prepare the food according to recipe directions. Pack it, still hot, in clean containers that have been washed in hot, soapy water and rinsed in scalding water. The food should reach ¹/₂ inch below the rim of the jars. Be sure that the jars are still hot enough that they will not crack when filled with hot food. Apply the lids and seal according to package directions.

2. Place a rack on the bottom of a large stainless-steel or enameled pot. Half-fill the pot with hot water. Place it over high heat.

3. Using tongs, lower the jars into the water, arranging them about 1 inch apart and 1 inch from the sides of the pot so that the water may circulate freely. Pour enough hot water over the jars to cover them by 2 inches. Cover the pot.

4. Bring the water to a boil, and continue boiling for the time specified in the recipe. Replenish the water from a teakettle if necessary.

5. Remove the jars from the bath, and set them on a wooden or cloth-covered surface at least 1 inch apart to cool.

FRESH CORN RELISH

Diverse as Americans are, most of them probably agree their favorite way to eat corn is on the cob, fresh from the garden, boiled quickly to bring out its natural sweetness and enhanced with just a thin coat of butter. It's always preferable, of course, to have your own corn patch, where you can pick individual ears at their peak and run them into the kitchen within minutes. But thousands of New Englanders rely on local, trusted farm stands for freshness.

A farsighted cook with an abundance of corn can plan to bring its flavor to the table year-round by canning. Cooked in quantity and properly preserved, this sweet-and-sour relish will be a mealtime delight for months on end.

Preparation time: about 1 hour

4 cups fresh corn kernels, cut from about 4 large ears of corn, or 1 pound frozen
1 cup finely chopped onion
1 red pepper, cored, seeded and finely chopped (about 1 cup)
1 green pepper, cored, seeded and finely chopped (about 1 cup)
2 cups thinly sliced celery

¼ cup dark brown sugar
1 tablespoon salt
1 tablespoon dry mustard
½ cup cider vinegar
½ cup water

1. If you are using fresh corn, cook the kernels in boiling water for about 1 minute; if you are using frozen corn, simply thaw it. Combine the corn with the onion, red and green peppers, and celery in a large nonreactive pot.

2. Add the brown sugar, salt, mustard, vinegar and water to the pot; stir to mix well. Bring the liquid to a boil; then reduce the heat to low, and simmer, covered, for about 15 minutes.

3. To preserve the relish, ladle it into sterilized jars and follow the directions for canning and sealing on page 151. Process the relish in a boiling-water bath for 15 minutes. This relish may also be served fresh; simply transfer it to a ceramic, glass or plastic bowl and refrigerate it. Serve chilled.

Makes about 2 quarts

In New England, the season for local vegetables is all too short. One way to prolong it—and use up the end-of-season bounty that simply can't be eaten all at once—is canning. This recipe for a vegetable melange, in your choice of sweet or sour, offers canning enthusiasts the opportunity to preserve the vestiges of a summer garden. What's more, the relish adds colors and flavors to the plate. Use any garden-fresh vegetables; the list that follows is merely a suggestion. The more varieties, the more interesting the relish. As those jars make their way, one by one, out of the pantry during the winter, you'll appreciate the variety.

Preparation time: about 14 hours

1. In a 5- to 6-quart enameled or stainless-steel pot, combine the tomatoes, cauliflower, cucumbers, onions, carrots and squash. Toss the vegetables well to mix them. Cover them with salt, then add enough water to fill the pot. Stir until the salt has dissolved. Cover the pot, and allow the vegetables to steep at room temperature for 8 to 10 hours.

2 pounds green tomatoes, cut into 1-inch pieces
1 head cauliflower, cut into flowerettes
1 pound cucumbers, peeled, seeded and cut into 1-inch pieces
1 pound onions, cut into 1-inch chunks
1 pound carrots, cut into ¹/₂-inch-thick rounds
1 pound yellow summer squash, cut into 1-inch pieces
¹/₂ cup salt

2. Drain the vegetables, rinse out the pot and return the vegetables to it. Add the vinegar, pickling spices, brown sugar (for sweet pickles) and water to cover. Stir to mix thoroughly.

3. Place the pot over high heat, and bring the liquid to a boil. Remove the pot from the heat immediately.

4. To preserve the pickles, follow the directions for canning and sealing on page 151. Process the jars in a boiling-water bath for 15 minutes.

2 cups cider vinegar
2 tablespoons mixed pickling spices
¹/₂ pound dark brown sugar (optional)

5. To serve the pickles without canning them, allow them to cool to room temperature, then refrigerate them in nonreactive containers, such as ceramic or glass bowls or jars.

6. Drain the pickles before serving them.

Makes about 3 quarts

NANCY BENZ'S DILL PICKLES

Nancy Benz's recipe for dill pickles produces the crunchiest, tastiest pickles I have ever eaten. Although Nancy no longer grows her own cucumbers in her Cape Cod garden—her enormous cucumber surplus one year was the impetus that started her pickling—she goes to a local farm stand early in the morning of the day she wants to can so she can select "the greenest and firmest."

Preparation time: about 1 hour (or longer, depending on the amount of cucumbers to be pickled)

6 cups white vinegar
6 cups water
²/₃ cup salt

Pickling cucumbers,
    unpeeled, whole or cut
    lengthwise in quarters
Dill sprigs
Garlic cloves, peeled and cut
    in half lengthwise
Powdered alum
Dill seed

1. Combine the vinegar, water and salt in a stainless-steel or enameled pot, and bring the liquid to a boil, stirring until the salt dissolves. Remove the vinegar solution from the heat, and reserve it.

2. Pack the pickles in clean, hot pint jars. For every pint jar add 1 sprig dill, 2 garlic pieces, ¹/₈ teaspoon alum and 2 teaspoons dill seed.

3. Fill the jars with the vinegar solution, making certain to cover the cucumbers completely. Seal the jars tightly. Immerse them in a boiling-water bath, and process them 5 minutes.

4. Remove the jars from the bath, and allow them to cool.

GERTRUDE WARD'S BREAD AND BUTTER PICKLES

A true New Englander, Gertrude Ward was born and has lived all her life in the small mill town of Orange, Massachusetts, at the eastern edge of the Berkshires. The Berkshires have hot summers and harsh winters, but the soil is good, and, like many others in Orange, Mrs. Ward has a small truck garden where she raises a profusion of vegetables and "cutting flowers." In August and September, when everything seems to come into fruit, her garden overflows with produce. So Mrs. Ward takes to her kitchen and her canning to have a merry assortment of pickles and conserves on her shelves and to give winter meals a bit of "zip," as she says.

Preparation time: about 4 hours

1. Place the cucumber and onion slices in a large bowl, and sprinkle them with the salt. Toss to distribute the salt as evenly as possible. Let the vegetables stand for 3 hours, then drain off the accumulated liquid. Rinse the vegetables in cold water, and drain them again.

9 pounds small, thin pickling cucumbers, cut in 1/4-inch-thick slices
2 pounds white onions, thinly sliced
3/4 cup coarse salt

2. In a large preserving kettle, combine the sugar, vinegar, water, mustard seed, turmeric, celery seed and cloves. Over moderate heat, stir until the sugar has dissolved. Increase the heat, and bring the liquid to a boil. Boil it for 5 minutes. Add the cucumbers and onions, lower the heat and simmer for 10 minutes, stirring occasionally. Do not overcook, or else the cucumber slices will not be crisp.

3. Ladle the vegetables, with the syrup, while still hot into sterilized pint canning jars, and seal the jars.

6 cups sugar
6 cups cider vinegar
2 cups water
3 tablespoons mustard seed
2 teaspoons turmeric
1 teaspoon celery seed
1 teaspoon ground cloves

Makes 12 pints

GERTRUDE WARD'S TOPSFIELD RELISH

Mrs. Ward modestly disclaims any particular talent for pickle and relish making. Yet for those who have tasted her products—and every year she used to produce between two and three dozen jars each of seven types of relish—they are truly an inspiration for us all. Her Topsfield Relish, a marvelous mix in texture and taste, is one of her very best.

Preparation time: 11 hours

4 pounds (*about 12 large*)
ripe tomatoes
4 pounds (*about 12 large*)
green tomatoes
2 large heads (*about 2
pounds each*) *green
cabbage, cored*
3 medium onions (*about
1¹/₂ pounds*), *peeled*
1 bunch celery (*about 2
pounds*), *trimmed of
green leaves*
3 large red peppers (*about
1¹/₄ pounds*), *cored and
seeded*
¹/₂ *cup coarse salt*

1. Cut the tomatoes (do not peel or seed them), cabbages, onions, celery and peppers into large chunks, and force them through the medium holes of a food or meat grinder into a large glass or ceramic bowl. Add the salt, and mix thoroughly. Cover the bowl loosely with plastic wrap, and let the vegetables stand overnight or for at least 8 hours.
2. Drain off all the liquid that has accumulated, and cover the vegetables with fresh water. Stir to rinse, then drain again.

4 *cups cider vinegar*
6 *cups sugar*
¹/₂ *teaspoon cinnamon*
¹/₂ *teaspoon ground cloves*
¹/₂ *cup mustard seed*

3. Transfer the vegetables to a large preserving kettle, and add the vinegar, sugar, cinnamon, cloves and mustard seed. Stir thoroughly. Set the kettle over moderate heat, and stir until the sugar has melted. Bring the liquid to a boil, lower the heat and simmer the vegetables, uncovered, for 2 hours, or until most of the liquid has evaporated and the mixture is fairly thick. Stir occasionally.
4. Immediately transfer the relish into hot, sterilized pint canning jars, and seal the jars.

Makes 12 pints

GREEN TOMATO PICKLE RELISH

I have no idea where this recipe originally came from, but I found it among the handwritten scraps of recipes my mother amassed during her lifetime. Since I always had too many green tomatoes in my garden ready to succumb to the first frost, I tried it out on my relish-fancying family, who quickly voted it one of their favorites. I particularly like to serve it with curries or as an accompaniment to cold meats, such as roast lamb or pork.

Preparation time: about 14 hours

1. Cut the tomatoes and onions into very thin slices. In a large stainless-steel, glass or enameled baking dish, place them in layers, sprinkling salt between the layers. Let the vegetables stand overnight.

12 pounds green tomatoes
9 pounds onions, peeled
1 cup coarse salt

2. Drain off all liquid that has accumulated, then cover the vegetables with fresh water. Drain them again.

3. In a 4- to 6-quart nonreactive kettle, heat the vinegar to the boiling point. Add the pepper, garlic, brown sugar, celery seed and salt, and stir until the brown sugar has dissolved. Spoon in the tomatoes and onions.

3 quarts cider vinegar
1 red pepper, cored, seeded and coarsely chopped
2 tablespoons minced garlic
3 pounds light brown sugar
1 tablespoon celery seed
2 teaspoons salt

4. Tie the cloves and cinnamon together in a double thickness of cheesecloth, and immerse the bag in the kettle. Bring the tomato mixture to a boil, lower the heat and simmer the mixture, partially covered, until the tomatoes become translucent, about 1 hour. Remove the bag of spices, and discard it.

2 tablespoons whole cloves
2 sticks cinnamon

5. Spoon the relish into sterilized 1-pint glass jars, and seal the jars.

Makes about 12 pints

CRANBERRY-APPLESAUCE CONSERVE

In early fall, cranberry growers flood most of the bogs in south-eastern Massachusetts with water to float the marble-size berries to the surface, then suck them up by means of sophisticated machinery. Not too long ago, the same bogs were worked dry, with laborers on their knees, using hand-held scoops with long wooden tines to dislodge the berries from their hiding places within the stubby green plants. Always the critical factor was time—the time between the berries' peak of ripeness and the descent of frost, which sometimes came before all the berries could be gathered. There's still the fear of frost, of course, but the flood waters temper the hard freeze, and the whole task is accomplished in a matter of days, not weeks.

New England cranberries and apples marry well in this recipe for a vibrantly red conserve, which I like to serve with meat. But add a little more sugar and it makes a splendid, wholesome dessert.

Preparation time: about 45 minutes

1½ pounds MacIntosh apples, peeled, cored and thinly sliced
1½ cups cranberries
¼ cup water
¾ cup light brown sugar

1. Place the sliced apples, cranberries and water in a heavy 2-quart saucepan. Add the brown sugar, and mix well. Bring the water to a boil. Lower the heat, and cover the pan. Simmer the fruit for 15 minutes.

2. Uncover the pan, toss the fruit briskly, and cook it, partially covered, for 10 minutes, or until the apple slices disintegrate easily when pressed with a spoon and most of the juices have evaporated.

2 teaspoons finely grated orange rind
¼ to ½ cup light brown sugar (optional)

3. With a wooden spoon, beat the fruit vigorously until it has broken down into a coarse puree. (If you prefer a really smooth applesauce, press it through a strainer or puree it in a food processor fitted with a steel blade.) Mix in the orange rind. Taste the conserve for sweetness, adding ¼ to ½ cup more sugar if desired. Stir well.

4. Serve the conserve at room temperature.

Makes about 3 cups

Very seldom can old recipes be used as written; tastes simply change too much from generation to generation. This remarkably simple recipe from *The New England Economical Housekeeper and Family Receipt Book*, by Mrs. E. A. Howland (New London, 1848), is a fine example. The original contained 50 percent more sugar, and everyone who tasted the result turned up their health-conscious noses. But the combination of the brown sugar with summer-fresh peaches proved quite irresistible, so I have made some adjustments and now heartily recommend this almost intact nineteenth-century receipt to anyone interested in preserving peaches. Try it on toast or muffins; try it pureed and blended with whipped cream as a "peach mousse" or try it as a filling for crêpes.

Preparation time: about 14 hours

1. Peel and cut the peaches into ½-inch-thick slices. Place them in a mixing bowl, and toss them with the brown sugar until the peaches and sugar are well combined. Cover the bowl loosely with plastic wrap, and allow the peaches to macerate for 12 hours.

2 pounds ripe peaches
2 cups packed dark brown sugar

2. Transfer the peaches and all the juices that have accumulated to a 3- to 4-quart saucepan. Set the saucepan over moderate heat, and bring the peaches to a boil. Skim off any froth that may form. Lower the heat, and simmer the peaches, uncovered, for 1½ to 1¾ hours, or until the juices have evaporated somewhat and thickened, and the peaches are very tender but still intact.

3. Remove the saucepan from the heat, and mix in the lemon juice. Spoon the peach preserve into sterilized jars, and seal them.

3 tablespoons strained fresh lemon juice

4. Store the peach preserve in a cool, dark space.

Makes about 3 cups

WILD BERRY JELLY: BEACH PLUM OR GRAPE

In the still warm days of September, a wonderful scent permeates the soft Atlantic air, coming in fits and starts on the small, gusting breezes. It is the heady aroma of ripening wild berries: rose hips, grapes and beach plums. And, like lemmings journeying to the sea, New Englanders take out their baskets and head for their favorite berry sources. Beach plums grow on scraggly bushes, close to the shore. Grapes can be found further inland in secretive bunches underneath tenacious vines. Rugosa roses grow at the edge of the beach, their cherry-red fruit provocatively large, bright and abundant, challenging the greed of the uninitiated jelly maker who is blissfully unaware of the myriad of tiny seeds and choke-like hairs contained within the berry that render it woefully difficult to use. (Hence no recipe here!)

For those of us who religiously undergo the ritual of September jelly making, grape and beach plum jellies are easy, although time-consuming. But, when all the little jars are filled and sitting, ruby red and crystal clear, in our larders, we are infinitely rewarded. No artificial pectin for us, just a mix of green and ripe berries to produce a natural pectin.

Preparation time: about 2 to 3 days for gathering, making the extract and boiling the jelly

Fresh beach plums or wild grapes, about 1/3 of them green and 2/3 fully ripe

1. Pick over the berries carefully, discarding moldy or bruised ones and removing any stems or leaves. The more berries you gather, the more jelly you will have. Ten cups of uncooked berries will produce roughly 4 cups of jelly, but the amount of jelly will vary because the amount of juice in the berries varies with the amount of rainfall during the growing season.

2. Pour water to the depth of 1/2 inch into an 8- to 10-quart nonreactive kettle. Add the berries. Bring the water to a boil over high heat. Cover the pot tightly, reduce the heat to moderately low and simmer for approximately 15 minutes, or until the berries have burst, exuding their juices.

3. Line a colander or strainer with several thicknesses of dampened cheesecloth or a linen towel, and suspend the colander over a large mixing bowl (or another nonreactive pot). Carefully transfer the berries and their juices to the colander, and allow the juices to

drain through to the bowl beneath. Do not squeeze or mash the berries in an effort to secure more extract; it will only cloud the finished jelly. Allow the berries to drain at least 2 hours, or as long as overnight.

4. When the berries have drained completely, you are ready to *Sugar* start making the finished product. (If you do not have time to progress immediately, the berry extract may be bottled, covered tightly and refrigerated for up to 2 weeks. It may also be frozen up to 1 month.) Make the jelly in small batches. A large pot containing a relatively small quantity of extract reduces the danger of boiling over. This permits you to boil the extract at a higher heat, producing more jelly in less time. For every 3 cups of extract, allow 2½ cups sugar. Place 3 cups of extract in a 5- to 6-quart nonreactive pot. Bring it to a boil. When it is boiling, add 2½ cups sugar, and stir until the sugar has dissolved. Boil the jelly, uncovered, over as high a heat as possible without its boiling over. Watch the pot carefully. When the jelly has reached a temperature of 220 degrees on a candy thermometer, or when it "sheets" when it drips off the tines of a fork (that is, the liquid, as it cools, starts to solidify and forms a thin layer or "sheet" between the tines), it is done. This generally takes about 25 minutes. Ladle it into hot sterilized jelly glasses, and seal the glasses.

XI
Desserts and Sweets

DESSERTS WITH A NEW ENGLAND ACCENT

Slumps, grunts, duffs, crisps, flummeries, fools, pandowdy. Odd-sounding names, but not so odd to the taste. What do they have in common? They're all desserts based on cooked fruit and some form of pastry.

Like so many old New England dishes, they feature simplicity of preparation and rely on ingredients at hand. For example, making flummery—a form of pudding, beloved in Britain, derived from a medieval sweetened gruel—is almost as easy as buttering bread. Apple pandowdy, similar to apple pie but just different enough to be refreshing, requires only the skill it takes to make and roll out a pastry short crust. The earliest duffs were served on sailing ships, whose cooks would make a pudding of flour, water, salt and yeast, boiled together in a bag; later, landlubbing housewives improved the dish by pouring the batter over fruit and baking it all together. And some desserts don't even require an oven. Apple slump, a stove-top delight, was the favorite dessert of author Louisa May Alcott, who borrowed the name for her home in Concord, Massachusetts.

APPLE PANDOWDY

Preparation time: about 1 1/2 hours

1. Preheat the oven to 350 degrees. Generously butter an 11-by-7-inch baking dish.
2. On a floured surface, roll the dough out to a thickness of 1/4 inch. Cut it into strips about 1/2-inch wide.

1/2 recipe Flaky Pie Pastry (see p. 183)

3. Arrange the apple slices in the bottom of the baking dish. Dribble the maple syrup evenly over the apples. Sift the brown sugar, cinnamon, salt, nutmeg and ginger into a bowl. Then sprinkle the mixture evenly over the apples. Position the pastry strips over the apples in a lattice pattern. Brush them with the melted butter.
4. Bake the pandowdy for 1 hour, or until the crust has browned and the apples are soft.

8 cups (about 3 pounds) sliced, cored and peeled apples (such as MacIntosh)
1/2 cup pure maple syrup
1/2 cup dark brown sugar
1/2 teaspoon cinnamon
1/4 teaspoon salt
1/2 teaspoon freshly grated nutmeg
1/2 teaspoon ground ginger
4 tablespoons unsalted butter, melted

5. Serve the pandowdy warm or at room temperature, topped with whipped cream if desired.

1 cup heavy cream, whipped (optional)

Serves 8

APPLE SLUMP

Preparation time: about 1 hour

6 cups (about 2 pounds)
  sliced, cored and peeled
  apples (such as
  MacIntosh)
1 cup dark brown sugar
1 teaspoon cinnamon
1 teaspoon freshly grated
  nutmeg
1/2 cup water

1. Place the apples in a 3-quart nonreactive saucepan. Add the brown sugar, cinnamon, nutmeg and water, and toss to mix. Cover the pan, and, over moderately high heat, bring the water to a boil. Stir the apples when they have begun to yield their juices. Reduce the heat to low.

1 1/2 cups flour
1/4 teaspoon salt
1 1/2 teaspoons baking
  powder
1/2 to 3/4 cup milk

2. Meanwhile, sift the flour, salt and baking powder into a mixing bowl. Add the milk a little at a time, stirring to blend. Add only enough milk for the mixture to come together into a soft ball.

3. With floured hands, form the dough into balls of about 1 tablespoon each, and position them side by side on top of the cooking apples. Cover the saucepan, and continue cooking on low heat until the dumplings have puffed and absorbed some of the apple juices, about 30 minutes. Remove the pan from the heat, and allow the slump to cool, uncovered, about 15 minutes.

1 cup heavy cream, whipped

4. Serve the apple slump in individual serving dishes warm or at room temperature, topped with whipped cream.

Serves 6

APPLE DUFF

Preparation time: about 1 hour

1. Preheat the oven to 325 degrees. Generously butter an 11-by-7-inch baking dish.

2. In a large skillet, combine the cider, sugar and tapioca over medium heat, and stir until the sugar dissolves. Add the apple slices, turning to coat them evenly. Bring the mixture to a boil. Reduce the heat to low, and cover the skillet. Continue cooking until the apple slices have softened partially, about 5 minutes. Remove them from the heat, and reserve them.

1 cup apple cider
1/2 cup sugar
2 tablespoons minute tapioca
6 cups (about 2 pounds) sliced, cored and peeled apples (such as MacIntosh)

3. In a mixing bowl, beat the egg whites with the salt until they form stiff peaks. In another bowl, beat the yolks and sugar together until they become very light in color. Beat the vanilla and almond extracts into the yolks and sugar.

4 eggs, separated
Pinch salt
2/3 cup sugar
1 teaspoon vanilla
1 teaspoon almond extract

4. Fold the flour into the yolks, mixing until all traces of white have disappeared. Gently fold the whites into the flour mixture.

2/3 cup flour

5. Transfer the apples to the buttered baking dish. Spoon the batter over them, spreading it in an even layer. Bake for 30 minutes, or until the cake topping is golden and a knife inserted in the middle of the cake layer comes out clean.

6. Just before serving, sprinkle the top of the Apple Duff with cinnamon sugar. Serve warm or at room temperature.

2 teaspoons cinnamon sugar

Serves 8

BLUEBERRY COTTAGE PUDDING WITH HARD SAUCE

By modern standards, "pudding" is a bit of a misnomer for this dessert, whose consistency is more like a coffee cake. A turn-of-the-century favorite, cottage pudding usually involved a simple cake batter poured over any fresh fruit or marmalade; the dessert was then baked. Often it was also topped with stewed fruit or hard sauce.

Although any berries may be used, fresh blueberries make an excellent cottage pudding, since baking enhances their simultaneously sweet and tart flavor. In both wild and cultivated varieties, they're abundant in summer not only in New England but throughout the United States, largely thanks to exports from Maine.

Preparation time: about 35 minutes

1. Preheat the oven to 425 degrees. Butter an 8-inch round baking pan that is at least 1½ inches deep.
2. In a bowl, cream the butter and sugar until the mixture is light and fluffy. Add the egg to the mixture, and beat until the mixture is well combined.

3 tablespoons unsalted butter
⅓ cup sugar
1 egg, beaten

1 cup flour
½ teaspoon salt
1 teaspoon baking powder
⅓ cup milk
1 teaspoon vanilla

3. Sift together the flour, salt and baking powder into a small bowl. Beat the dry ingredients into the butter mixture in two parts alternately with the milk, beating well after each addition. Stir in the vanilla.

1 cup fresh blueberries, washed and picked over

4. Spread the blueberries in the bottom of the baking pan, and, with a rubber spatula, scrape the batter evenly over them. Do not stir. Bake the "pudding" for 20 minutes, or until a straw inserted in the center comes out clean. Set the "pudding" on a rack to cool.

1 recipe Hard Sauce (see p. 196)

5. Cut the "pudding" into wedges and serve it warm, topped with Hard Sauce.

Serves 6 to 8

INDIAN PUDDING

Early on, Indian Pudding became a New England favorite. Based on the English concept of puddings and the American staples cornmeal and molasses, Indian Pudding requires little else of the cook than a good, strong crock and a good, hot oven. Although traditional recipes call for many hours of baking, 3 hours are sufficient—especially if you're among those who prefer this dessert soft and a little runny.

Preparation time: about 3½ hours

1. Preheat the oven to 300 degrees. Generously butter a 2-quart baking dish.

2. In a large saucepan, heat the milk, molasses and butter, stirring to blend them. Over moderate heat, bring them slowly to just under a boil, stirring occasionally.

4 cups milk
2/3 cup unsulphured molasses
3 tablespoons unsalted butter

3. Meanwhile, combine the cornmeal, sugar, cinnamon, nutmeg, ginger and salt, and sift them into a bowl.

4. When the milk and molasses are close to, but not quite, boiling, gradually stir in the cornmeal mixture. Cook, mixing constantly so that no lumps form, until the pudding thickens enough to hold its shape when stirred.

1 cup yellow cornmeal
1/2 cup sugar
1 teaspoon cinnamon
1 teaspoon freshly grated nutmeg
1 teaspoon ground ginger
1/2 teaspoon salt

5. With a rubber spatula, scrape the pudding into the buttered baking dish. Add the milk, but do not mix it in; let it float on top. Bake the pudding, uncovered, for 1 hour without stirring. Then stir in the milk, and bake 2 hours longer.

2 cups milk

6. Serve the Indian Pudding warm with whipped cream or ice cream, if desired.

1 cup heavy cream, whipped, or 1 quart vanilla ice cream, softened (optional)

Serves 8 to 10

BLUEBERRY CRISP

Heresy or not, I prefer Blueberry Crisp to blueberry pie. Its satisfyingly crunchy topping seems to enhance the berries—wild or cultivated—better than any pie crust. Blueberry Crisp was first brought to my attention by a friend in New Hampshire, one of those true Yankees who wouldn't think of having anything on her table that she hadn't either grown herself or scavenged from the woods. Her desserts all had those fascinating New England names like "slumps," "grunts" and "crisps," which, as a transplanted New Yorker, I found absolutely intriguing; I was never quite certain what I was getting.

Preparation time: about 45 minutes

2 pints fresh blueberries,
  washed and picked over
¾ cup sugar
½ teaspoon freshly grated
  nutmeg
2 tablespoons strained fresh
  lemon juice
3 tablespoons grated orange
  rind

1. Preheat the oven to 350 degrees.

2. In a large bowl, combine the blueberries, sugar, nutmeg, lemon juice and orange rind. Toss to mix well. Set the mixture aside while you prepare the topping.

¾ cup flour
½ cup dark brown sugar
6 tablespoons unsalted
  butter, softened

3. In another bowl, mix the flour and brown sugar until they are well blended. Add the butter, and rub it into the flour mixture with your fingertips until the mixture attains a crumbly consistency.

4. Transfer the blueberries to a 1- to 2-quart deep baking dish, spreading them out evenly. Spread the brown sugar mixture evenly on top.

5. Bake the crisp, uncovered, for 30 minutes, or until the berries are bubbling and the topping appears crisp.

1 cup heavy cream, plain or
  whipped

6. Serve the crisp hot from the oven, with plain or whipped cream.

Serves 8

FOUR-BERRY PUDDING

New England is berry land. The first settlers were overwhelmed with the profusion of wild strawberries, raspberries, blackberries and blueberries. These berries can still be found wild, particularly the further north one goes, although urban expansion is fast usurping their habitat. Fortunately, all are extensively cultivated and available for consumption—with the exception of the tiny red and white currants. These tart berries were once common but are rare now, prohibited from cultivation in New England because they play host to a parasitic fungus that proves lethal to our beautiful white pine.

Preparation time: about ¹/₂ hour plus chilling

1. Pour the berries into a 2- to 3-quart nonreactive saucepan. Add the water and 1 cup sugar. Stir to mix. Set the pan over low heat. When the berries start to exude their juices, increase the heat to moderately high. Boil for 15 minutes, stirring occasionally. Taste the berries and the syrup for sweetness, adding up to 1 more cup sugar if desired. Stir until any added sugar is dissolved.

4 cups assorted berries such as raspberries, blueberries, blackberries, strawberries or currants, washed and picked over
¹/₄ cup water
1 to 2 cups sugar, according to tartness of berries

2. Allowing approximately 2 teaspoons butter per slice of bread, generously butter six to eight slices of bread on one side each. (The number of slices depends on the bread's size and shape and the shape of the dish in which you will be placing it. You want to have three layers of bread.)

6 to 8 slices stale white bread
12 to 16 teaspoons (¹/₄ to ¹/₃ cup) unsalted butter, softened

3. Cutting the slices of bread to fit, place a layer of bread, buttered side down, on the bottom of a 9-inch soufflé dish or its equivalent. Ladle one-third of the stewed berries and their juices over the bread. Repeat this two more times, ending with a layer of berries.

4. Cover the pudding with plastic wrap, and refrigerate it overnight or for at least 6 hours.

5. Serve the pudding cold or at room temperature, accompanied by a pitcher of cream.

1 cup heavy cream

Serves 8

SUMMER BERRY PUDDING

Everybody loves berries in any combination in the summer. They seem to beat the heat. Here's another variation on a theme, and variety, they say, is the spice of life.

Preparation time: 2¹/₂ hours

1/4 cup minute tapioca

1/2 cup sugar

2 cups water

2 tablespoons strained fresh
lemon juice

1/4 teaspoon salt

1 pint strawberries, washed
and picked over

1/2 cup sugar

1 cup blueberries, washed
and picked over

1 cup raspberries, picked
over

1 cup heavy cream,
whipped, or 1 recipe
Mock Zabaglione Sauce
(see p. 195)

1. In a saucepan, combine the tapioca, sugar, water, lemon juice and salt, and stir to mix them. Set the pan over medium heat and, stirring constantly, bring the mixture to a boil. Immediately remove it from the heat to cool and thicken.

2. Meanwhile, in a food processor fitted with a steel blade, or in a shallow bowl with a fork, puree the strawberries with the sugar. When the pudding has cooled to room temperature, fold the puree, along with the blueberries and raspberries, into the tapioca, mixing until all the berries are evenly distributed. Transfer the pudding to a serving bowl, cover it with plastic wrap and refrigerate it for at least 2 hours or until you are ready to serve.

3. Serve the pudding chilled, accompanied by a sauceboat of whipped cream or Mock Zabaglione Sauce.

Serves 8

MAPLE BREAD PUDDING WITH RUM SAUCE

For the Pilgrims, thrift was not so much a virtue as a necessity: They simply could not afford to let anything go to waste. That trait has remained with New Englanders—especially the cooks—through the centuries. One of the resources they have learned to stretch to its utmost is cheap, plentiful bread. Stale bread is transformed into stuffings, crumb toppings (used in so many seafood dishes) and even desserts, such as flummery and bread pudding.

This rich version has a particularly New England flavor, since it is sweetened with our local maple syrup and served with an optional sauce made from the favorite beverage of our sea captains, rum. Any type of bread without a savory seasoning (such as caraway seeds) will do; a good French or Italian bread is ideal, and a few handfuls of pumpernickel will make a visually attractive marbled pudding. To prevent an undesirable salty taste, it is essential to use unsalted butter in both the pudding and the sauce.

Preparation time: about 1 1/2 hours

1. Preheat the oven to 350 degrees. Generously butter a 2-quart baking dish.

2. Place the bread in a large bowl. In another, combine the butter, milk, cream, maple syrup and flavoring, eggs, sugar, raisins, walnuts, cinnamon and nutmeg. Stir until the ingredients are thoroughly blended. Pour the mixture over the bread, and toss until all the pieces of bread are moist.

3. Transfer the mixture to the baking dish. Bake the pudding, uncovered, in the middle of the oven until the top is golden brown, about 1 hour.

10 ounces stale bread, broken into large pieces
1/2 cup unsalted butter, melted
2 cups milk
1 cup heavy cream
1 cup pure maple syrup
1 tablespoon maple flavoring
3 eggs, well beaten
1 cup dark brown sugar
1 cup seedless raisins
1 cup coarsely chopped walnuts
1 teaspoon cinnamon
1 teaspoon freshly grated nutmeg

4. Spoon individual servings of the warm bread pudding onto dessert plates, and ladle Rum Sauce over the top.

Rum Sauce (optional; see p. 196)

Serves 8

BOSTON CREAM PIE

There are many versions of Boston Cream Pie. Some are filled with custard, others with jelly or jam. Some are sprinkled with confectioners' sugar; others are given a quick glaze of chocolate. All, however, use a basic yellow cake. Why the dessert is called a "pie" remains a mystery. One can only speculate that its inventor had no cake pans and resorted to pie plates instead. Traditionally, the baker deals with the slanted sides of the pie pans by inverting the bottom layer and having the smaller edges of the cake rounds meet in the middle, where the filling holds them together.

Preparation time: about 1 1/2 hours

1/3 cup unsalted butter,
   softened
3/4 cup sugar

1. Preheat the oven to 375 degrees. Generously butter two 8-inch cake pans (or, more traditionally, pie pans) and dust them with flour, knocking out any excess.

2. With an electric mixer, or by hand, cream the butter with the sugar until the mixture is light and fluffy.

1 1/2 cups cake flour
2 teaspoons baking powder
1/4 teaspoon salt

3. Combine the flour, baking powder and salt in a strainer, and sift the ingredients into a bowl.

2 eggs
1/2 cup milk
1 teaspoon vanilla

4. In another bowl, beat the eggs together with the milk and vanilla.

5. In three parts, add the flour to the butter mixture alternately with the egg mixture. Mix until the batter is smooth.

6. Divide the batter between the two prepared cake or pie pans. Bake the cakes about 20 minutes, or until a knife inserted in the center comes out clean.

7. Turn the cakes immediately out on a rack to cool.

1/4 cup milk
2 tablespoons cornstarch
2 eggs, well beaten

8. Pour the milk into a small bowl, and add the cornstarch. Stir until the cornstarch has dissolved. Add the eggs, and mix well.

3/4 cup light cream, scalded
Pinch salt

9. Stirring constantly, pour the cream in a slow, steady stream into the cornstarch mixture. Stir in the salt. Return the mixture to the saucepan in which the cream was scalded, and cook the custard over moderate heat, stirring constantly, until it thickens.

1 teaspoon vanilla

10. Remove the saucepan from the heat, and beat in the vanilla. Cool the custard to room temperature.

3 tablespoons confectioners'
   sugar
Chocolate Glaze (recipe
   follows)

11. Make certain each cake layer is flat; cut off any irregularities with a serrated knife. Place one layer on a plate, upside down, and spread it evenly with the custard filling. Top with the second layer. Using a strainer, dust the confectioners' sugar evenly over the top, or, with a metal spatula, with Chocolate Glaze (recipe follows), allowing some to dribble down the sides.

Makes 1 (8-inch, 2-layer) "pie"

1. In a small saucepan over very low heat, melt the chocolate with the butter, and stir until the mixture is smooth.

3 (1-ounce) squares
  semisweet chocolate
2 tablespoons unsalted
  butter

2. Remove the pan from the heat, and add the cream, stirring constantly. Set the mixture aside to cool completely.

¹/₄ cup light cream

3. Sift the sugar over the chocolate, and beat until smooth. Add the salt and vanilla, and stir to mix.

¹/₂ cup confectioners' sugar
Pinch salt
¹/₂ teaspoon vanilla

MINCE PIE

Preparation time: about 1¹/₂ hours

1. Preheat the oven to 450 degrees.
2. On a lightly floured surface, roll out slightly more than one-half the pastry very thin. Line a 9-inch pie plate with it.
3. Spread the mincemeat evenly in the prepared pie shell.
4. Roll the remaining pastry into a circle, and drape it over the pie. Trim the excess dough, and seal the top and bottom crusts securely together. Cut several slashes in the top to allow steam to escape.

1 recipe Flaky Pie Pastry
  (see p. 183)
3 cups homemade
  Mincemeat (see p. 174)

5. In a small bowl or cup, combine the egg and cream. Lightly brush the surface of the pie with the mixture.

1 egg, beaten
2 tablespoons light cream

6. Bake the pie 20 minutes. Reduce the heat to 350 degrees, and bake 20 to 25 minutes more.
7. Serve the pie warm or at room temperature, accompanied by Hard Sauce (see p. 196) or slices of cheddar cheese.

Hard Sauce (see p. 196)
Cheddar cheese slices

Makes 1 (9-inch) pie

MINCEMEAT

Mince pie at Christmas is an ancient custom brought to the New World from England, where, along with plum pudding, mince pie is part and parcel of Yuletide tradition. The early settlers in New England used to include venison or even beef tongue in their mincemeat. This recipe calls for venison, but feel free to substitute round of beef. Whatever meat you choose, please don't have it ground. Chopping produces a much better texture, and, with a food processor, it doesn't take much time at all.

Preparation time: about 3 hours

1 pound venison steak (or top round of beef)

1. Trim the steak of all fat and gristle. Cut it crosswise into slices ¼-inch thick. Place the slices in the freezer 20 to 30 minutes, or until they are partially (not totally) frozen. Transfer the meat in two batches to the bowl of a food processor fitted with a steel blade. Whirl, pulsating on and off, until the meat is finely chopped. (Be careful not to overchop it.) Or finely chop the meat by hand. As each batch is done, transfer it to an 8- to 10-quart kettle.

2. To the meat in the kettle, add the suet, citron, candied orange peel, raisins, currants, orange rind, white and brown sugars, apples, salt, cinnamon, allspice, cloves, mace and nutmeg. With your hands or two large wooden spoons, toss until the ingredients are thoroughly mixed. Pour in the cider and port, and stir to blend the ingredients.

3. Set the kettle over moderate heat, and bring the liquid to a boil. When it boils, lower the heat. Simmer the mincemeat, partially covered, for 1 hour. Remove the lid, and simmer 1 hour more.

1/2 pound ground suet
1 (4-ounce) container candied citron, finely chopped
1 (4-ounce) container candied orange peel, finely chopped
1 (15-ounce) package seedless raisins
2 (10-ounce) packages dried currants
3 tablespoons grated orange rind
1 cup white sugar
1 cup brown sugar
3 pounds apples, peeled, cored and coarsely chopped
1 teaspoon salt
1 teaspoon cinnamon
1 teaspoon allspice
1 teaspoon ground cloves
1 teaspoon ground mace
1 teaspoon freshly grated nutmeg
2 cups sweet cider
2 cups tawny port

4. Transfer the mincemeat to sterilized 1-quart jars, filling them three-quarters full. (A well-filled 9-inch pie will require about 3 cups mincemeat.) Spoon 3 tablespoons Cognac or rum into each jar, and stir to mix.

15 tablespoons Cognac or dark rum

5. Seal the jars, and store them in a cool place for at least 1 week before using the mincemeat, to allow the flavors to develop.

Makes 15 cups or enough for 5 (9-inch) pies

SARA'S GREEN TOMATO AND APPLE PIE

The growing season is short in New England, even in the southern states. The rule of thumb most gardeners follow is that it is safe to plant after Memorial Day—and expect the first killing frost by mid-October. By mid-September, then, we New Englanders are forced to acknowledge that the bulk of our still green tomatoes will never ripen in time. Usually, they find their way into pickle relish of one sort or another (see p. 157). But here is a most unusual way to make use of green tomatoes, even for New England. The recipe was given to me years ago by a lady with a very deft hand with apple pies, who lived in Gloucester on Cape Ann, north of Boston. She just took her talent a little bit further and combined apples from her small orchard with the last green tomatoes in her garden.

Preparation time: about 1 hour

1 pound (*about 2 large*) *apples, such as Golden Delicious*
1 pound green tomatoes
³/₄ cup seedless raisins

1. Preheat the oven to 450 degrees.
2. Peel and core the apples, and cut them into ¹/₂-inch-thick slices. Transfer them, as they are sliced, to a mixing bowl. Remove any residual stems from the tomatoes, and cut them into ¹/₂-inch-thick wedges as similar in shape to the apple slices as you can manage. Combine the tomatoes and raisins with the apples.

¹/₂ cup dark brown sugar
¹/₃ cup white sugar
¹/₄ teaspoon ground cloves
1 teaspoon cinnamon
2 tablespoons minute tapioca
1 egg, beaten

3. Sprinkle the brown and white sugars, cloves, cinnamon and tapioca over the fruit, and toss to distribute them thoroughly. Add the beaten egg, and toss again.

1 recipe Flaky Pie Pastry (*see p. 183*)

4. On a lightly floured surface, roll out slightly more than one-half the pastry very thin. Line a 9-inch pie plate with it.
5. Pack the tomato-apple mixture into the pie shell, mounding it in the center. Moisten the rim of the pastry with water.
6. Roll the remaining pastry into a circle, and drape it over the pie. Trim the excess dough, and seal the top and bottom crusts securely together. Cut several slashes in the top crust to allow steam to escape.

7. In a small bowl or cup, combine the egg and cream. Using a pastry brush, lightly coat the surface of the pie with the mixture.

8. Bake the pie 20 minutes. Reduce the heat to 350 degrees, and bake 20 to 25 minutes longer, or until the crust is nicely brown.

9. Serve the pie hot or at room temperature, plain or accompanied by Mock Zabaglione Sauce.

Makes 1 (9-inch) pie

1 egg, beaten
2 tablespoons light cream

1 recipe Mock Zabaglione Sauce (optional; see page 195)

FRESH PUMPKIN PIE
WITH OR WITHOUT GINGER OR NUTS

Pumpkin pie is, of course, one of *the pies* whose presence on the table is a must at Thanksgiving. In our family, my son demands one nearly every week, or so it seems to me, and polishes it off at breakfast if he didn't quite manage to finish it the night before. I try to vary it a bit at times, with such additions as chopped crystallized ginger or nuts or different proportions of spices. Whatever I do, it doesn't seem to matter to him. He just keeps eating it.

Preparation time: about 1¹/₂ hours

1. Preheat the oven to 425 degrees. On a lightly floured surface, roll out the pastry very thin. Line a 9-inch pie plate with the pie dough. Set it in the refrigerator to chill.

¹/₂ recipe Flaky Pie Pastry (see page 183)

2. Break the eggs into a large mixing bowl. With an electric beater, beat them until they are frothy. Add the brown sugar and corn syrup, and continue beating until the ingredients are well mixed. Beat in the salt, cinnamon, ginger and cloves. Add the pumpkin puree and cream, and continue beating until the ingredients are thoroughly blended.

3 eggs
¹/₂ cup dark brown sugar
¹/₂ cup dark corn syrup
¹/₂ teaspoon salt
1 teaspoon cinnamon
1¹/₂ teaspoons ground ginger
¹/₄ teaspoon ground cloves
1¹/₂ cups fresh Pumpkin Puree (see page 178; or use canned pumpkin or squash puree)
1 cup heavy cream

½ cup coarsely chopped
  crystallized ginger
  (optional)
½ cup toasted chopped
  walnuts or pecans
  (optional)

½ cup heavy cream,
  whipped (optional)

3. If desired, stir in the ginger or nuts, or both.
4. Pour the batter into the prepared chilled pastry shell. Bake the pie in the oven for 1 hour. Set it on a rack to cool.

5. Serve the pie either warm or at room temperature, accompanied by dollops of whipped cream, if desired.

Makes 1 (9-inch) pie

PUMPKIN PUREE

Even in New England, most people resort to using canned pumpkin puree when a recipe calls for pumpkin. Nonetheless, it doesn't take much effort to make the Real Thing, particularly if it appeals to the cook to make good use of the remains of the Halloween pumpkin.

Preparation time: 1½ hours

1 pumpkin

1. Preheat the oven to 350 degrees.
2. Cut the pumpkin in half crosswise. Scrape out the seeds and threads. Place the halves, cut side down, on a jelly roll pan, preferably Teflon-coated. Bake the pumpkin until it feels tender when pierced with a knife, about 1 hour, depending on its size.
3. Remove the pumpkin from the oven, and set it aside to cool. When it is cool enough to handle, cut the skin off with a sharp paring knife. Place the pumpkin pieces in a food processor fitted with a steel blade, and whirl until they are nicely pureed (or use a food mill).

Makes about 3 cups puree from a 3-pound pumpkin

PEACH AND BLUEBERRY ALMOND TART

Tarts are not traditional in New England, but pies certainly are, and blueberries and peaches are summer staples in the Northeast. If you are a stickler for authenticity, use a large pie plate instead of a tart pan.

Preparation time: about 1½ hours

1. Preheat the oven to 400 degrees.
2. Place the flour and sugar in the bowl of a food processor fitted with a steel blade. Whirl for a second or two to mix them. Add the butter, in pieces, the salt and the vanilla, and whirl until a self-adhering ball of dough has formed. (Or mix the dough by hand, or with an electric mixer.)

1 cup flour
⅓ cup sugar
½ cup unsalted butter, softened
¼ teaspoon salt
¼ teaspoon vanilla

3. Taking small pieces of dough, pat them over the bottom of an 11-inch tart pan with removable sides (or an 11-inch pie pan) until the bottom is completely covered with the dough. (Do not put any dough up the sides.) Distribute it as evenly as possible; it should be about ⅛-inch thick.
4. Place the pastry in the oven and bake it 10 minutes, or until the crust is a faint golden brown.
5. Remove the pastry from the oven, and set it on a rack to cool. Do not turn the oven off.
6. Drop the almonds into the bowl of a food processor fitted with a steel blade. Whirl until the almonds are ground into fine particles. Do not overblend, or the almonds will become oily. Add the sugar, egg and cinnamon, and blend until a smooth paste has formed.

1¼ cups sliced almonds
½ cup sugar
1 egg
½ teaspoon cinnamon

7. When the tart pastry has cooled completely, use a rubber spatula to spread the paste, which will be sticky, evenly over the crust. (Dip the spatula frequently in water to facilitate the spreading.)
8. Arrange the peach halves in a concentric circle around the outer edge of the tart. Sprinkle the peaches with 2 tablespoons sugar, and dot them with 2 tablespoons of butter.

5 ripe peaches (about 1½ pounds), peeled, cut in half lengthwise and pitted
2 tablespoons sugar
2 tablespoons unsalted butter, cut in small pieces

9. Transfer the tart to the oven, and immediately reduce the heat to 375 degrees. Bake the tart for 25 minutes.

1 1/2 cups cultivated
  blueberries, picked over
2 tablespoons sugar
1 tablespoon butter

10. Remove the tart from the oven, and spoon the blueberries decoratively in the center and in and around the peaches, wherever there is space on top of the almond paste. Sprinkle the berries with the remaining 2 tablespoons sugar, and dot them with the remaining 1 tablespoon butter. Return the tart to the oven, and bake it another 15 minutes.

11. Remove the tart from the oven, and run a knife around the edge to loosen the sides. Lift off the sides of the pan. Transfer the tart, still resting on the bottom section of the pan, to a rack to cool. (Do not remove the tart if it has been made in a pie pan; let it cool in the pan.)

1 cup heavy cream

12. Serve the tart, cut in wedges, at room temperature accompanied by a pitcher of heavy cream or, if you prefer, a bowl of whipped cream.

Serves 8

CRANBERRY-LEMON MOUSSE PIE

Preparation time: about 3 hours

1. Preheat the oven to 350 degrees.

2 cups (about 1/2 pound)
  crushed gingersnaps
1/4 cup sugar
1/2 cup unsalted butter,
  melted

2. Combine the gingersnaps and sugar in a mixing bowl. Drizzle the butter over the top, and stir until the butter is completely absorbed. Press the mixture onto the sides and bottom of a pie plate 9 1/2 inches wide and 2 1/2 inches deep. Bake the pie crust for 15 minutes. Remove it from the oven, and let it cool.

1/4 cup water
1 envelope gelatin

3. Pour the water into a small saucepan. Sprinkle the gelatin over its surface. When the gelatin has softened, place the saucepan over low heat, and stir until the gelatin has dissolved. Remove it from the heat, and reserve it.

4. Place the cranberries, sugar and water in an enamel-covered or stainless-steel saucepan. Bring the water to a boil over high heat, stirring constantly until the sugar dissolves. Reduce the heat to low. Simmer, uncovered, for 5 minutes, or until the berries just begin to pop. Remove the pan from the heat, drain the berries (discarding the liquid) and allow them to cool. Pick out 16 whole, still perfect berries, and set them aside. With a sharp knife, coarsely chop the remaining berries, and reserve them.

1 cup cranberries
1/2 cup sugar
1 cup water

5. In a mixing bowl, beat the egg yolks with the sugar until they are light and lemon-colored. Beat in the reserved gelatin and lemon juice. Place the mixture in the refrigerator until it has thickened to the consistency of mayonnaise.

3 egg yolks
1 cup sugar
1/2 cup strained fresh lemon juice

6. Fold the whipped cream into the lemon mixture.

1 cup heavy cream, whipped

7. In another bowl, beat the egg whites until they are stiff. Fold them into the cream-and-lemon mixture, mixing until no traces of white remain. Fold in the chopped cranberries.

3 egg whites
1/3 cup sugar

8. Spoon the mixture into the prepared crust, swirling the surface attractively. Arrange the reserved whole cranberries decoratively on the top as a garnish.

9. Refrigerate the pie until the filling is set, about 2 hours.

Makes 1 (9 1/2-inch) pie

MAPLE-WALNUT PIE

New England's Maple-Walnut Pie is a kissin' cousin of the South's Pecan Pie, but the subtle maple flavoring makes it particularly special. Maple syrup, one of New England's prize products, is made from the spring-running sap of the sugar maple tree, and it takes approximately forty gallons of sap to produce one gallon of syrup. The finest, and most delicate, syrup is graded "Fancy." "A" comes next, followed by "B" and "C," all of them becoming progressively stronger in flavor and deeper in color. ("C" is blended with sugar syrup to produce a cheaper "pancake and waffle" syrup.) Ideally, Maple-Walnut Pie should be made with grade B syrup; the more intense flavor will permeate the pie nicely.

1. Preheat the oven to 375 degrees.
2. In a large bowl, beat the eggs for a minute or two, or until they start to thicken. Still beating, gradually pour in the maple syrup. Add the flour, butter, salt and vanilla, and beat until the ingredients are well combined. Mix in the walnuts.

4 eggs
1 1/2 cups maple syrup,
  preferably grade "B"
2 tablespoons flour
3 tablespoons unsalted
  butter, melted
1/4 teaspoon salt
1 teaspoon vanilla
3/4 cup walnuts

1/2 recipe Flaky Pie Pastry
  (see page 183)

3. On a lightly floured surface, roll out the pastry dough very thin. Line a 9-inch pie plate with it. Pour the maple mixture into the prepared 9-inch pie shell, and set it on a jelly roll pan or cookie sheet. Bake the pie for 40 minutes. (The filling, which may appear soft, will solidify as it cools.)

1 cup heavy cream, whipped

4. Serve the pie warm or at room temperature, cut in wedges topped with generous dollops of whipped cream.

Makes 1 (9-inch) pie

RHUBARB AND STRAWBERRY PIE

After a long, harsh New England winter, nothing bespeaks spring so much as the arrival in the garden of the first shoots of rhubarb. Depending on the weather, rhubarb is ready to be harvested by the end of May, sometimes even earlier. As much as I love it by itself, I always save a few shoots to combine with the first strawberries, which appear around the middle of June. Sometimes I'll just stew them together; other times they go into a pie. Either way, they're a wonderful combination. Don't ever nibble on the rhubarb leaves, though. They're very poisonous.

Preparation time: about 1 1/4 hours

1. Preheat the oven to 425 degrees
2. Drop the rhubarb pieces into a large bowl. Add the strawberries, and toss gently with your hands to mix. Sprinkle the fruit with the brown sugar, tapioca and salt. Mix gently but thoroughly. Add the beaten eggs, and toss until all the fruit is well coated.

1½ pounds rhubarb stalks (trimmed of leaves), cut into 1-inch lengths
1 pint strawberries, washed and hulled
1½ cups dark brown sugar
2 tablespoons minute tapioca
Pinch salt
2 eggs, well beaten

3. Divide the pastry into one slightly larger and one slightly smaller sections. On a floured board, roll out the larger portion as thin as possible. Fit it into a 9-inch pie plate, leaving a ½-inch overlap. Roll out the remaining pastry and, with a sharp knife, cut decorative slits in the center to allow steam to escape during the baking.
4. Transfer the rhubarb and strawberry mixture into the pie plate, mounding it in the center. Moisten the edges of the pastry shell. Top with the second piece of pastry, and crimp the edges together, cutting off any excess.
5. Brush the top of the pie with the cream, and sprinkle it with the sugar.
6. Bake the pie for 20 minutes at 425 degrees; then lower the heat to 350 degrees, and bake it 30 minutes longer. Serve the pie hot or at room temperature.

1 recipe Flaky Pie Pastry (see p. 183)

3 tablespoons heavy cream
1 teaspoon white sugar

Makes 1 (9-inch) pie

FLAKY PIE PASTRY

Lard has been the staple shortening for New England's pastry since pie making began in these parts because there were more pigs from which to render fat than cows to produce butter. Lard is not the best ingredient if you are concerned with cholesterol levels, but it certainly produces a light and flaky crust.

Preparation time: about 45 minutes

2 cups flour
1/2 teaspoon salt

1/2 cup lard, well chilled
2 tablespoons unsalted
  butter, well chilled
1/4 cup ice water

1. Place the flour and salt in the bowl of a food processor, and whirl briefly to blend them.

2. Cut the lard and butter into small chunks, and drop them on top of the flour in the processor. Cover the machine, and pulsate on and off only until the mixture resembles coarse meal. Add the water slowly through the feed tube, with the machine going, and stop the moment the pastry starts adhering to itself. Do not overblend the pastry, or it will toughen.

(To make the dough by hand, sift the flour and salt into a large bowl. Cut the lard and butter into small pieces, drop them into the flour, and, with two knives, your fingers, or a pastry cutter, work the shortening into the flour until the mixture resembles coarse meal. Drizzle the water over the mixture, and mix only until the pastry starts adhering to itself. Remove it from the bowl, and knead it briefly.)

3. Remove the pastry from the processor, and divide it into two portions, equal in size (for one-crust shells), or one slightly larger than the other (for two-crust pies). Flatten the portions slightly, wrap them in plastic wrap and refrigerate them until you are ready to use them, but at least 30 minutes.

4. When you are ready to prepare the pie crusts, place one round of pastry (the larger one, for a two-crust pie) on a sheet of lightly floured waxed paper. Sprinkle a bit of flour on top of the dough, and cover it with another sheet of waxed paper. (This makes rolling thin pastry a lot easier!) Starting at the center, and using light strokes, roll the pastry into a round about 1 1/2 inches larger in diameter than the pie plate and about 1/8-inch thick. Carefully remove the waxed paper, and gently line the pie plate, taking care not to stretch the dough. Trim the edge evenly with a sharp knife.

5. Roll out the second portion of pastry, using it either for another pie shell or as a lid for a two-crust pie. Refrigerate the pastry until you are ready to use it.

Makes enough pastry for 2 (9-inch) pie shells or 1 2-crust (9- or 9 1/2-inch) pie

STRAWBERRY SHORTCAKE

The first settlers in the Northeast were astonished and delighted by the profusion of strawberries growing wild. Roger Williams, founder of Rhode Island, reported in 1643: "This berry is the wonder of all the fruits growing naturally in those parts. . . . In some parts where the *Natives* have planted, I have many times seen as many as would fill a good ship. . . ."

Strawberries in New England mean strawberry shortcake in June, our strawberry harvest season. In recent years, the cake in the shortcake has evolved into—heresy—sponge cake. But for shortcake purists, the cake must be made out of baking powder–biscuit dough, sweetened according to taste, but heavy on the butter so that, true to its name, the cake is very short.

Preparation time: about 40 minutes

1. Preheat the oven to 450 degrees. Generously butter an 8-inch cake pan or cast-iron "spider."
2. In the bowl of a food processor fitted with a steel blade, place the flour, ¼ cup sugar (or up to ½ cup, if you prefer a sweeter cake), baking powder, salt and nutmeg. Whirl for 5 seconds to mix the dry ingredients. Cut the butter into ¼-inch-thick slices, and drop them on top of the flour mixture in the bowl of the processor. Whirl until the butter has been cut into the dry ingredients and the mixture resembles coarse meal. With the motor still running, pour the cream through the feed tube. Whirl until the mixture adheres to itself and forms a soft dough.

(To make the dough by hand, sift the flour, sugar, baking powder, salt and nutmeg into a large bowl. Cut the butter into small pieces, drop them into the flour mixture, and, with two knives, your fingers or a pastry cutter, work the butter into the flour until the mixture resembles coarse meal. Drizzle the water over the mixture, and mix only until the pastry starts adhering to itself.)

3. Immediately turn the dough out onto a lightly floured surface, and knead it briefly. Pat the dough into the prepared pan until it fits the circular form compactly. Bake the cake for 15 minutes, or until it is light brown.

2 cups flour
¼ to ½ cup sugar
1 tablespoon baking powder
½ teaspoon salt
⅛ teaspoon freshly grated nutmeg
½ cup unsalted butter, well chilled
½ cup light cream

2 tablespoons unsalted
  butter, softened

1 quart strawberries, hulled
  and washed
1/2 cup sugar
2 tablespoons strained fresh
  lemon juice

2 cups heavy cream,
  whipped

4. Remove the shortcake from the oven. Run a knife around the edge of a pan to loosen it, and turn it out on a rack. While the cake is still warm, cut it in half horizontally with a serrated knife.

5. Spread each cut side of the cake with 1 tablespoon butter.

6. Wash the food processor and dry it.

7. Place half the berries in the bowl of the food processor, fitted with a steel blade. Whirl until they are coarsely chopped. Add the sugar and lemon juice, and whirl 10 seconds, or until the berries are pureed. Add the remaining berries, and whirl briefly to chop them. Do not overblend them. The sauce should have the texture of crushed berries.

8. The shortcake may be presented in either of two ways. It may be assembled whole, which is more dramatic but far harder to carve at the table, or it may be cut into wedges first and served in individual portions. Whichever you prefer, ladle half the crushed strawberries over the bottom layer of shortcake (either left whole or cut into 8 pie-shaped wedges), cut side up, cover with the top layer of cake (or wedges), cut side down, top with the remaining strawberries and embellish with generous dollops of whipped cream.

Serves 8

PUMPKIN CAKE

Jacques Cartier called native pumpkins *gros melons* when he discovered them in the St. Lawrence area in 1584. The words, however, were translated in England into "pompions," or pumpkins. The settlers who followed Cartier to the New World soon took up cultivating the exclusively American vegetable; they planted it between cornstalks in the fields to use space efficiently while balancing the quality of the soil at the same time.

New Englanders still like their pumpkins, in many forms. This lovely, dense cake, with its pumpkin base, will remain moist for several days.

Preparation time: about 2 hours

1. Preheat the oven to 350 degrees. Generously butter and flour a 10-inch tube pan, shaking out any excess flour.

2. In a strainer, combine and sift the flour, salt, nutmeg, ginger, cinnamon and baking soda, and stir the ingredients into a mixing bowl.

3 cups flour
1 teaspoon salt
1 teaspoon freshly grated nutmeg
1 teaspoon ground ginger
2 teaspoons cinnamon
2 teaspoons baking soda

3. With an electric mixer, beat the oil and sugar until they are well combined. Add the eggs, one at a time, beating well after each addition. Beat in the pumpkin puree.

4. Using a wooden spoon, or the electric mixer on a very slow speed, mix the dry ingredients into the oil mixture in three parts, blending well each time.

1 cup vegetable oil
3 cups sugar
4 eggs
2 cups fresh Pumpkin Puree (see p. 178) or 1 (15-ounce) can pureed pumpkin

5. Add the vanilla, and mix well. Fold in the raisins and walnuts. With a rubber spatula, scrape the batter into the prepared cake pan.

1 teaspoon vanilla
1 cup seedless raisins
1/2 cup coarsely chopped walnuts

6. Place the pan in the oven, and bake the cake 1¼ to 1½ hours, or until a toothpick inserted in the center comes out clean. Set it on a cake rack to cool for 15 minutes. When the cake is cool enough to handle, run a knife around the edges of the pan. Remove the cake from the pan, inverting it onto the rack to cool completely.

7. Using a strainer, sift the confectioners' sugar delicately over the cake.

1/4 cup confectioners' sugar

Makes 1 (10-inch round) tube cake

GROTON ALMOND-APPLE CAKE

The rolling, undulating land north and west of Boston is some of Massachusetts's most beautiful. Bisected by rivers, dotted with lakes, its long-range vistas are made the more attractive by the peaceful presence of church steeples, set seemingly at random in village clusters, silhouetted white against the green background.

In the spring the hills and valleys are a wonderland of apple orchards whose pale pink blossoms hold promise of the abundance to be: Macs, Cortlands, Spencers and the wonderfully crisp, juicy Macouns. The recipe that follows is quick and easy to prepare; it's best made with Macouns, but if you can't find them—and their shelf life is brief—substitute the reliable (non-native) Granny Smiths.

Preparation time: about 1¼ hours

1. Preheat the oven to 350 degrees. Generously butter a 9½-inch springform cake pan.
2. In a mixing bowl, whip the butter until it is creamy. Slowly beat in the sugar.

½ cup unsalted butter, softened
¾ cup sugar

3. Place a strainer over the mixing bowl. Put the flour, baking powder and salt in it, and sift the ingredients through. Remove the strainer and, beating hard, mix until the flour is thoroughly incorporated.

1 cup flour
1 teaspoon baking powder
¼ teaspoon salt

4. Drop the eggs and almond extract into the batter, and beat until the ingredients are well mixed. With a rubber spatula, scrape the batter into the prepared springform pan. Smooth the top if necessary.

2 eggs
1 teaspoon almond extract

5. Arrange the apple slices decoratively in concentric circles on top of the batter. Sprinkle them with the lemon juice, almonds and cinnamon sugar.
6. Bake the cake on a rack in the center of the oven for 1 hour.

2 to 3 Macoun apples, peeled, cored and sliced thin
2 tablespoons strained fresh lemon juice
¼ cup finely chopped almonds
2 tablespoons cinnamon sugar

7. Remove the sides from the cake pan. Serve the Groton Almond Apple Cake hot from the oven, cut in wedges, accompanied by generous dollops of whipped cream.

1 cup heavy cream, whipped

Serves 8

GINGERED PUMPKIN CHEESECAKE

This Pumpkin Cheesecake is a fine example of New England thrift. It was improvised by a "maiden aunt," to use my mother's expression, an exceptional cook who lives at the foot of a rain-eroded Berkshire mountain in western Massachusetts. She was making a traditional cheesecake for dinner. Finding some leftover pumpkin puree in her full larder, she decided to add it to the cheese batter, in the interest of both economy and experimentation. We all should have such luck!

Preparation time: about 2¹/₂ hours

1. In a mixing bowl, combine the gingersnaps, pecans and brown sugar. Dribble the butter over the mixture, toss well until the crumbs start to adhere to each other, and press the mixture onto the sides and bottom of a 9¹/₂-inch springform pan. Place the pan in the freezer, and chill the crust for 15 minutes.
2. Preheat the oven to 350 degrees.

³/₄ cup crushed gingersnaps (about 8 to 12, depending on their size)
¹/₂ cup finely chopped pecans
¹/₂ cup brown sugar
¹/₄ cup unsalted butter, melted

3. Drop the cream cheese into the bowl of a food processor fitted with a steel blade or the bowl of an electric mixer. Whirl until it is creamy. Add the eggs, one at a time, whirling after each addition. Add the sugar, and blend briefly. Add the cinnamon, nutmeg and salt, and whirl until they are blended in. Blend in the pumpkin puree. Add the crystallized ginger, and whirl briefly to distribute the pieces.
4. With a rubber spatula, scrape the contents of the processor into the chilled crust.
5. Bake the cheesecake in the center of the oven for 50 minutes. It may seem slightly soft. Do not be concerned; it will solidify as it cools.
6. Cool the cheesecake, in its pan, on a rack for 1 to 2 hours.

3 (8-ounce) packages cream cheese, softened
4 eggs
1 cup sugar
2 teaspoons cinnamon
¹/₂ teaspoon freshly grated nutmeg
¹/₂ teaspoon salt
1¹/₂ cups Pumpkin Puree (see page 178) or canned pumpkin
¹/₃ cup finely chopped crystallized ginger

1 cup heavy cream, whipped
3 tablespoons finely chopped
    crystallized ginger

7. Gently combine the whipped cream with the ginger, mixing only until the ginger is well distributed. Run a knife around the edge of the springform pan to facilitate removal of its side. Swirl the heavy cream decoratively over the surface of the cake.

Serves 10 to 12

ROSE WATER–CURRANT CAKE

Many old English recipes call for the flavoring agent rose water, an intensely rose-imbued solution made from steaming the petals of roses. (Because it is widely used in Middle Eastern cuisine still, rose water is readily available in specialty stores carrying Middle Eastern produce.) It is an unusual flavor, to say the least, but a very pleasant one, as this traditional pound cake recipe will prove.

Preparation time: about 2 hours

1. Preheat the oven to 300 degrees. Generously butter a 9-by-5-inch loaf pan. Line it crosswise with waxed paper cut to fit, allowing 4 or 5 inches extra on both long sides to use as handles later, when you extract the cake.

1 cup unsalted butter,
    softened
1 1/2 cups sugar

2. In a large bowl, cream the butter until it is light and creamy. Add the sugar by the quarter-cupful, beating continuously.

5 eggs

3. Add the eggs one at a time, beating well after each addition.

2 cups cake flour, sifted

4. Slowly beat in the cake flour, a half cup at a time. Beat only until the flour is completely incorporated.

2 tablespoons rose water
1 teaspoon vanilla

5. Add the rose water and vanilla, and blend well.

3/4 cup dried currants

6. With a spatula, add in the currants, mixing until they are well distributed. Scrape the batter into the prepared loaf pan, spreading it out into the corners. Give the pan a sharp rap on the counter to eliminate any air bubbles.

7. Bake the cake for 1 1/2 hours, or until a straw inserted in the middle comes out clean.

8. Run a knife across the ends of the loaf pan to loosen the cake. Using the wax paper handles, lift the cake out of the pan and transfer it to a rack to cool.

Makes 1 (9-by-5-inch) loaf

GINGERY GINGERBREAD

When European explorers and traders sailed for the Far East in the fifteenth century, ginger was one of the coveted spices they brought back. Seagoing New Englanders also loved it—it's one of the most commonly mentioned spices in seventeenth century recipes—for its medicinal purposes as well as for its flavor. Ginger's benefits include warding off seasickness, and sailors on long ocean voyages carried ginger cakes and cookies to help them through rough weather. Today some over-the-counter motion-sickness remedies use ginger as their base, and New England pleasure-boaters have been known to carry bags of commercially baked gingersnaps down below—just in case.

Preparation time: about 1 1/2 hours

1. Preheat the oven to 350 degrees. Generously butter a 9-inch square baking pan.
2. In a mixing bowl, beat the egg and sugar together until the mixture is light in texture. Add the butter, beating constantly.

1 egg
1/2 cup sugar
*8 tablespoons unsalted
  butter, melted and cooled*

2½ cups flour
2 teaspoons baking soda
1 tablespoon ground ginger
1 teaspoon cinnamon

½ cup unsulphured
  molasses
½ cup honey
1 cup hot water

⅓ cup finely chopped
  preserved stem ginger

1 cup heavy cream, whipped

3. In a strainer, combine the flour, baking soda, ginger and cinnamon, and sift them into a bowl.

4. In a 2-cup measuring container or small pitcher, mix the molasses, honey and hot water until they form a smooth blend.

5. Add the dry and liquid mixtures alternately, one-third at a time, to the butter mixture. With a wooden spoon, beat vigorously until the ingredients are well blended.

6. Stir the chopped ginger into the batter, breaking up any clumps. Continue stirring until the ginger is evenly distributed. With a rubber spatula, scrape the batter into the prepared baking pan. Bake the gingerbread for 1 hour, or until a knife inserted in the center comes out clean. Set the pan on a rack to cool.

7. Cut the gingerbread into 3-inch squares. Serve it either warm or at room temperature, topped with whipped cream.

Makes 9 squares

SOFT AND SPICY HERMITS

Preparation time: about 1 hour

1. Preheat the oven to 350 degrees. Generously butter the sides of a 10-by-15-inch jelly roll pan. Line the pan with waxed paper, allowing 3 inches at each end for overlap (which will act as handles and facilitate the removal of the hermits from the pan). Generously butter the waxed paper.

2. Combine the flour, cinnamon, allspice, nutmeg, baking soda and salt in a strainer, and sift them into a mixing bowl.

3 cups flour
2 teaspoons cinnamon
1 teaspoon allspice
½ teaspoon freshly grated
  nutmeg
1 teaspoon baking soda
½ teaspoon salt

3. In another mixing bowl, combine the butter and the sugar, and cream them until they are light and fluffy.

1/2 cup unsalted butter, melted
1 cup sugar

4. Combine 1/2 cup milk with the molasses, and stir until they are well blended. In three parts, add the spice and flour mixture to the butter alternately with the molasses-milk mixture, beating well after each addition. The batter should be stiff but spreadable. If it seems too sticky, add up to 1/4 cup more milk. Beat the batter until it is smooth.

1/2 to 3/4 cup milk
1/2 cup unsulphured molasses

5. Sprinkle the raisins (and nuts, if desired) over the batter, and mix thoroughly. Spoon the batter into the prepared jelly roll pan, spreading it out as evenly as possible with a rubber spatula.

3/4 cup seedless raisins
3/4 cup chopped walnuts (optional)

6. Bake for 25 minutes for moist, chewy hermits, or 30 minutes for a more cakelike cookie.

7. Remove the pan from the oven and, on a clean surface, turn it over while still hot. Immediately peel off the waxed paper. Allow the hermits to cool; then cut them into 2-by-3-inch squares.

Makes about 25 cookies

JOE FROGGERS

No doubt every New England grandma for the last three centuries or so has had her own recipe for molasses cookies. Among the best are Joe Froggers, attributed to—as legend has it—an old man named Uncle Joe and the frogs that lived in his pond. Besides molasses, the other key ingredient in the cookies is rum. As the legend explains, the cookies were invented when someone gave Uncle Joe a jug of rum, and he added some of it to the batter for the molasses cookies he baked as a thank-you gift.

Molasses and rum were major cargoes shipped on two of the three legs of the infamous Triangle Trade. Molasses, the residue produced when sucrose is extracted from sugar cane, came to New England from the West Indies. The prices it would bring didn't make it worth shipping to Europe, but thrifty Yankee sea captains snapped it up and brought it home, for it was cheaper than sugar. Once the molasses was unloaded, its place in the cargo ships was taken by New England rum, which was shipped to Europe and

Africa. Many of the black slaves who were traded for rum ended up in the West Indies, where they worked on the sugar plantations and produced molasses.

Like tea, molasses was heavily taxed by the British before the Revolution, although, as far as we know, there was no Boston Molasses Party. But, many years later, molasses did play the lead role in what must surely be a unique event in history: the Great Molasses Flood. On an unseasonably warm day in January 1918, a four-story silo on Commercial Street, along the waterfront in Boston's North End, exploded. It had been filled with molasses, and the explosion let loose a 50-foot-high tidal wave that traveled through the city streets at 35 miles an hour, killing a dozen people. Some North End residents swear they can still smell molasses rising from the sidewalks on hot summer days.

This version of Joe Froggers is a little heavier on the rum than some, but the amount may be reduced if you prefer. Although the basic cookie calls for a doughy round, you may let your imagination run to other forms. And if by chance you have a frog-shaped cookie cutter, what could be better?

Preparation time: about 1 hour, plus chilling

2 cups flour
1 teaspoon ground ginger
¹/₄ teaspoon ground cloves
¹/₄ teaspoon freshly grated
  nutmeg
¹/₄ teaspoon allspice
¹/₂ teaspoon salt

1. Sift the flour, ginger, cloves, nutmeg, allspice and salt together into a large bowl.

¹/₂ cup unsulphured
  molasses
¹/₂ teaspoon baking soda

2. In a small bowl, combine the molasses and the baking soda, stirring briskly with a fork. Set the mixture aside until it stops foaming.

5 tablespoons unsalted
  butter
¹/₂ cup sugar
¹/₂ cup dark rum

3. In a large bowl, cream the butter and sugar together until they are light and fluffy. Beat in the molasses mixture. When the ingredients are well blended, add the rum and stir well.

4. With a wooden spoon, beat the flour and spices into the molasses mixture, one-half cup at a time. When all the flour has been incorporated, form the dough into a round about 1-inch thick, and wrap it in plastic wrap. Refrigerate it for several hours or overnight.

5. Preheat the oven to 375 degrees, and generously butter two baking sheets.

6. Remove the dough from the refrigerator and, with a rolling pin, roll it out about ⅓-inch thick. Using a 3-inch round cookie cutter, cut the dough into rounds, and place them at least 2 inches apart on the baking sheets. Bake the cookies about 10 minutes, or until they are puffed and the edges slightly browned. While still warm, remove them with a spatula, and set them on a rack to cool.

7. Repeat until all the dough has been used up, rerolling the scraps as necessary.

Makes about 30 (3-inch) cookies

MOCK ZABAGLIONE SAUCE

New Englanders love their fruit and berries. What they don't grow themselves, they either buy or gather. There are all kinds of sauces to enhance fruit, but this is one of my favorites. Unlike its namesake, it is easy to make—and you would swear it was the real, time-consuming thing!

Preparation time: about 10 minutes

1. In a chilled bowl, whip the cream until stiff peaks form. Set the bowl aside.

2. In a mixing bowl, beat the egg yolks for 2 minutes, or until they are thick and lemon-colored. Beat in the confectioners' sugar, and continue to beat for 2 additional minutes. Add the Marsala, and beat for 1 minute. Fold in the reserved whipped cream, mixing it lightly until it is thoroughly incorporated.

3. Hold the zabaglione in the refrigerator until you are ready to serve it. It will hold well for 2 hours.

Makes 3 cups

1 cup heavy cream

2 egg yolks
1 cup confectioners' sugar, sifted
4 tablespoons sweet Marsala wine

RUM SAUCE

Preparation time: about 10 minutes

¹/₂ cup unsalted butter
1¹/₂ cups confectioners'
* sugar, sifted*
1 egg yolk, beaten
¹/₂ cup dark rum

1. In a small saucepan, melt the butter over low heat. Add the confectioners' sugar, and whisk until all the sugar has been absorbed. Add the egg yolk and, stirring, cook for 1 minute. Remove the pan from the heat, and add the rum. Blend well.

Makes about 1 cup

HARD SAUCE

Preparation time: about 10 minutes

¹/₂ cup unsalted butter,
* softened*
1 cup confectioners' sugar,
* sifted*
2 tablespoons dark rum or
* brandy*

1. In a small bowl, cream the butter well. Beat in the confectioners' sugar, and mix until smooth and well blended. Beat in the rum or brandy.

Makes about ³/₄ cup

Bibliography

SEVENTEENTH-CENTURY ANGLO-AMERICAN COOKERY

Anderson, Jay A. "A Solid Sufficiency: An Ethnography of Yeoman Foodways in Stuart England." Ph.D. diss., University of Pennsylvania, 1971.

Aylett, Mary, and Ordish, Olive. *First Catch Your Hare*. London: MacDonald, 1965.

Ayrton, Elisabeth. *English Provincial Cooking*. New York: Harper & Row, 1980.

Bradford, William. "Bradford's Letter Book," *Massachusetts Historical Society Collections*, ser. I, vol. III, pp. 27–76. Boston: Massachusetts Historical Society, 1794.

————. *Of Plimoth Plantation, 1620–1647*. Edited by Samuel Eliot Morison. New York: Alfred A. Knopf, 1952.

————. "Verses." In *A Dialogue, or, Third Conference Between Some Young Men Born in New England and Some Ancient Men Which Came Out of Holland and England, Concerning the Church and the Government Thereof*. Edited by Charles Deane, 61–78. Boston: John Wilson & Son, 1870.

Braudel, Fernand. *The Structures of Everyday Life*. New York: Harper & Row, 1981.

Brett, Gerard. *Dinner Is Served*. London: Rupert Hart-Davis, 1968.

Carson, Jane. *Colonial Virginia Cookery*. Williamsburg: Colonial Williamsburg Foundation, 1968.

Cosman, Madeline. *Fabulous Feasts: Medieval Cookery and Ceremony.* New York: George Braziller, 1976.

Crawford, Mary C. *Social Life in Old New England.* New York: Grosset & Dunlap, 1914.

Cummings, Richard. *The American and His Food.* New York: Arno Press, 1970.

Dawson, Thomas. *The Good Huswifes Jewell.* (London, 1587); Ann Arbor: University Microfilms, 1975.

————. *The Second Part of the Good Huswifes Jewell.* (London, 1597); Ann Arbor: University Microfilms, 1975.

Dow, George F. *Every Day Life in the Massachusetts Bay Colony.* Boston: Society for the Preservation of New England Antiquities, 1935.

Drummond, J. C., and Wilbraham, Anne. *The Englishman's Food.* London: Jonathan Cape, 1960.

Earle, Alice Morse. *Customs and Fashions in Old New England.* New York: Charles Scribner's Sons, 1893.

————. *Home Life in Colonial Days.* New York: Macmillan, 1899.

Erath, Sally L., ed. *The Plymouth Colony Cookbook.* Plymouth, Mass.: The Plymouth Antiquarian Society, 1957.

Farb, Peter, and Armelagos, George. *Consuming Passions: The Anthropology of Eating.* Boston: Houghton Mifflin, 1980.

Gerard, John. *The Herball or General Historie of Plantes. Gathered by John Gerard of London, Master in Chirurgerie.* (London, 1597); Norwood, N.J.: Walter J. Johnson, 1974.

The Good Huswifes Handmaide for the Kitchin. (London: Richard Jones, 1594); Ann Arbor: University Microfilms, 1975).

Hackwood, Frederic W. *Good Cheer: The Romance of Food and Feasting.* New York: Sturgis & Walton, 1911.

Hale, William H. *The Horizon Cookbook and Illustrated History of Eating and Drinking through the Ages.* New York: American Heritage, 1968.

Hartley, Dorothy. *Food in England.* London: MacDonald, 1954.

Henish, Bridget. *Fast and Feast: Food in Medieval Society.* University Park, Penn.: Pennsylvania State University Press, 1976.

Hess, Karen, ed. *Martha Washington's Booke of Cookery.* New York: Columbia University Press, 1981.

Hooker, Richard J. *Food and Drink in America: A History.* Indianapolis: Bobbs-Merrill, 1981.

James, Sydney V. *Three Visitors to Early Plymouth.* Plymouth, Mass.: Plimoth Plantation, 1963.

Leighton, Ann. *Early American Gardens.* Boston: Houghton Mifflin, 1970.

Love, W. DeLoss. *The Fast and Thanksgiving Days of New England.* Boston: Houghton Mifflin, 1895.

Lorwin, Marge. *Dining with William Shakespeare*. New York: Atheneum, 1976.

M., W. *The Compleat Cook and A Queens Delight* (first published as *The Queens Closet Opened*). (1655); London: Prospect Books, 1984.

Markham, Gervase. *The English Huswife* (from *Countrey Contentments of the English Huswife*). (London, 1623); Montreal: McGill-Queen's University Press, 1896.

May, Robert. *The Accomplisht Cook*. London: J. Winter, 1671.

Morton, Thomas. *The New English Canaan*, Charles Francis Adams, ed. Boston: The Prince Society, 1883.

Murrell, John. *A New Book of Cookerie, Wherein is Set Forth the Newest and Most Commendable Fashion for Dressing or Sowcing, Eythere Flesh, Fish, or Fowl . . . Set Forth by the Observation of a Traveller*. (London, John Browne, 1615); New York: DaCapo Press, 1972.

"Plymouth Colony Wills and Inventories Transcriptions, vol. I; 1621–1654." Research Library, Plimoth Plantation, Plymouth, Mass. Typescript.

Oxford, Arnold W. *English Cookery Books to the Year 1850*. London: Holland Press, 1979.

Proportion of Provisions Needfull for Such as Intend to Plant Themselves in New-England, for One Whole Year. London: Fulke Clifton, 1630.

Quayle, Eric. *Old Cook Books*. New York: E. P. Dutton, 1978.

Rutman, Darrett B. *Husbandmen of Plymouth*. Boston: Beacon Press, 1967.

Sass, Lorna. *To the Queen's Taste: Elizabethan Feasts and Recipes Adapted for Modern Cooking*. New York: Metropolitan Museum of Art, 1976.

Simmons, Amelia. *American Cookery*. (Hartford: Hudson & Goodwin, 1796); Johnsburg, N.Y.: Buck Hill Association, 1966.

Tusser, Thomas. *Five Hundred Points of Good Husbandry*. London: James Tregaskis & Son, 1931.

W., A. *A Book of Cookrye*. (London: Edward Allde, 1591); Norwood, N.J.: Walter J. Johnson, 1976.

Warner, Richard, ed. *Antiquitatis Culinariae; or Curious Tracts Relating to the Culinary Affairs of the Old English*. (London, 1791); London: Prospect Books, n.d.

Wilson, C. Anne. *Food and Drink in Britain: From the Stone Age to Recent Times*. London: Constable, 1973.

Winthrop, John. *The History of New England from 1630–1649*. James Savage, ed. Boston: Little, Brown, 1853.

Young, Alexander. *Chronicles of the First Planters of the Colony of Massachusetts Bay from 1623 to 1636*. Boston: Charles C. Little and James Brown, 1846.

_____. *Chronicles of the Pilgrim Fathers*. Boston: Charles C. Little and James Brown, 1841.

Axtell, James, ed. *The Indian Peoples of North America.* New York: Oxford University Press, 1981.

Bennett, M. K. "The Food Economy of the New England Indians." *Journal of Political Economy* 63, no. 5 (October 1955): 369–97.

Champlain, Samuel de. *Voyages of Samuel de Champlain, 1604–1618.* (Paris: Claude Collet, 1632); New York: Barnes & Noble, 1967.

Densmore, Frances. *How Indians Use Wild Plants for Food, Medicine and Crafts* (originally published as *Uses of Plants by the Chippewa Indians*). (American Bureau of Ethnology, 1928); New York: Dover, 1974.

Erichsen-Brown, Charlotte. *Use of Plants for the Past Five Hundred Years.* Aurora, Ontario: Breezy Creek Press, 1979.

Gookin, Daniel. *Historical Collections of the Indians in New England.* (Boston: Belknap and Hall, 1792); New York: Arno Press, 1972.

Harrington, M. R., *The Indians of New Jersey.* New Brunswick, N.J.: Rutgers University Press, 1966.

Heath, Dwight B., ed. *A Journal of the Pilgrims at Plymouth: Mourt's Relation.* New York: Corinth Books, 1963.

Josselyn, John. *New-Englands Rarities.* (London: G. Widdowes, 1672); Boston: Massachusetts Historical Society, 1972.

Lindholdt, Paul J., ed. *John Josselyn, Colonial Traveler: A Critical Edition of "Two Voyages to New-England."* Hanover: University Press of New England, 1988.

Mangelsdorf, Paul C. *Corn: Its Origin, Evolution and Improvement.* Cambridge, Mass.: Harvard University Press, 1974.

Parker, A. C., "Iroquois Uses of Maize." *New York State Museum Bulletin* 44 (November 1910).

Sagard, Fr. Gabriel. *The Long Journey to the Country of the Hurons.* Ontario: Champlain Society, 1939.

Speck, Frank. *Penobscot Man.* New York: Octagon Books, 1976.

——— and Dexter, Ralph W. "Utilization of Marine Life by the Wampanoag Indians of Massachusetts." *Journal of the Washington Academy of Sciences* 38, no. 8 (August 15, 1948): 257–65.

Tantaquidgeon, Gladys. *Folk Medicine of the Delaware and Related Algonkian Indians.* Harrisburg: Pennsylvania Historical and Museum Commission, 1977.

Waugh, F. W. "Iroquois Foods and Food Preparation." *Geological Survey, Memoir 86.* Ottawa: Government Printing Bureau, 1916.

Williams, Roger. *A Key into the Language of America.* New York: Russell & Russell, 1973.

Willoughby, Charles C. *Antiquities of the New England Indians.* Cambridge: Peabody Museum, 1935.

Winthrop, John, Jr. "Indian Corne." *New England Quarterly* 10, no. 1 (1937).

Winship, George P., ed. *Sailors' Narratives of the Voyages along the New England Coast, 1524–1624.* New York: Burt Franklin, n.d.

Wood, William. *New England's Prospect.* (London: John Bellamie, 1634.) Edited by Alden T. Vaughan. Amherst: University of Massachusetts Press, 1977.

Index

The Plimoth Plantation New England Cookery Book is available from the publisher for $10.95 in a paperback edition and $19.95 in hardcover. If you would like to order one or more copies, please write to—

The Harvard Common Press
535 Albany Street
Boston, Massachusetts 02118

When ordering, please include a check for the full amount plus shipping and handling charges of $3.00 for a single book and $.50 for each additional copy. If the order is to be sent to a Massachusetts address, add 5 percent sales tax.

The Harvard Common Press is also publisher of the following cookbooks, all available by mail-order. (With your payment, please include shipping and handling charges and Massachusetts tax, if applicable.)

The Blue Strawbery Cookbook:
  Cooking (Brilliantly)
  Without Recipes
by James Haller
$8.95 paper
ISBN 0-916782-05-0

Another Blue Strawbery:
  More Brilliant Cooking
  Without Recipes
by James Haller
$8.95 paper
ISBN 0-916782-46-8

The Book of Chowder
by Richard J. Hooker
$7.95 paper
ISBN 0-916782-10-7

The Citrus Cookbook
by Josephine Bacon
$8.95 paper
ISBN 0-916782-42-5

The Farmers Market Cookbook
by Fran Jurga Garvan
$8.95 paper
ISBN 0-916782-30-1

The Gardner Museum Café
  Cookbook
by Lois Conroy
$8.95 paper
ISBN 0-916782-71-9

The Abbey Cookbook
by Hans Bertram
$10.95 paper
ISBN 0-916782-26-3

The Pillar House Cookbook
by David Paul Larousse and
  Alan R. Gibson
$14.95 paper
ISBN 1-55832-005-9

A Taste for All Seasons:
  A Celebration of American
  Food
by the chefs of ARA Fine
  Dining in association with
  David Paul Larousse
$24.95 hardcover
ISBN 1-55832-020-2